DARK PSYCHOLOGY:

How to Use the NLP Secret Methods of Manipulation for Social Influence, Emotional Persuasion, Deception and Mind Control - A Guide Based on Hypnosis and Brainwashing Techniques

By: David Drive

Copyright © 2019 – David Drive
All rights reserved

The content contained within this book may not be reproduced, duplicated or transmitted without direct written permission from the author or the publisher.
Under no circumstances will any blame or legal responsibility be held against the publisher, or author, for any damages, reparation, or monetary loss due to the information contained within this book. Either directly or indirectly.

Legal Notice:
This book is copyright protected. This book is only for personal use. You cannot amend, distribute, sell, use, quote or paraphrase any part, or the content within this book, without the consent of the author or publisher.

Disclaimer Notice:
Please note the information contained within this document is for educational and entertainment purposes only. All effort has been executed to present accurate, up to date, and reliable, complete information. No warranties of any kind are declared or implied. Readers acknowledge that the author is not engaging in the rendering of legal, financial, medical or professional advice. The content within this book has been derived from various sources. Please consult a licensed professional before attempting any techniques outlined in this book.

By reading this document, the reader agrees that under no circumstances is the author responsible for any losses, direct or indirect, which are incurred as a result of the use of information contained within this document, including, but not limited to errors, omissions, or inaccuracies.

Table of Contents

Introduction 1
Chapter 1: Neuro-Linguistic Programming 6
    The History of Neuro-Linguistic Programming 8
    The Key Concepts of Neuro-Linguistic Programming 11
    Manipulation Technique #1: In-Depth Learning Strategies . 21
    Manipulation Technique #2: Manipulating Beliefs 24
    Takeaways 26
Chapter 2: The Dark Triad 28
    Concepts of the Dark Triad: Narcissism 29
    Concepts of the Dark Triad: Machiavellianism 32
    Concepts of the Dark Triad: Psychopathy 36
    Why Should You Care About The Dark Triad? 43
    The Dark Triad: Recap 45
Chapter 3: Persuasion and Deception 48
    Psychology, Robert Cialdini, and the Six Principles of Persuasion 50
    The Six Principles of Persuasion: Authority 51
    The Six Principles of Persuasion: Reciprocity 54
    The Six Principles of Persuasion: Likeability 58
    The Six Principles of Persuasion: Commitment and Consistency 60
    The Six Principles of Persuasion: Social Proof 62
    The Six Principles of Persuasion: Scarcity 64
    Deception 66

Takeaways 68

Chapter 4: Mind Control **70**
What Is The Difference Between Mind Control, Hypnosis, And Brainwashing? 71
Mind Control: Myths vs. Reality 75
Manipulation Technique #3: Mind Control, Storytelling, and Controlling the Narrative 79
Takeaways 87

Chapter 5: Hypnosis **89**
The History of Hypnosis 90
Manipulation Technique #4: The Hypnotic Trance 94
Manipulation Technique #5: Choose Your Targets Wisely .104
Takeaways 107

Chapter 6: Brainwashing **108**
The History of Brainwashing 109
Manipulation Technique #6: Isolation, Criticism, and Identity Formation 116
Manipulation Technique #7: Managing Your Target's Expectations 123
Takeaways 127

Chapter 7: Case Studies **128**
Case Study #1: NLP Techniques in Modern Medicine 130
Case Study #2: Thought Reform in Communist China 135
Case Study #3: The CIA Brainwashing Experiments 143
Takeaways 148

Conclusion **150**

Introduction

Congratulations on choosing *Dark Psychology: How to Use the NLP Secret Methods of Manipulation for Social Influence, Emotional Persuasion, Deception, and Mind Control*.

The following chapters will discuss manipulation techniques involving neuro-linguistic programming, mind control, hypnosis, and brainwashing, as well as the concepts and principles that make them up, including the personality traits of the Dark Triad, persuasion, and deception.

The final chapter will also include three detailed case studies in order to better understand the concepts covered in the book. Chapters will also contain specific methods of manipulation that can be used in any situation and can even be combined with each other to become even more powerful.

Every technique introduced in this book will build on information that has been previously discussed so that learning each new concept will feel like a natural progression and will not be confusing or difficult to understand. By the time you have reached the end of this book, you will have gained a solid understanding of the concepts and techniques that make up dark psychology and manipulation, and you will be ready to try out these techniques in the real world on any target that you choose.

If this book is your first introduction to dark psychology and manipulation, then welcome! The information presented in the following chapters might seem overwhelming at times, but stick with it, and you will find that you have gained valuable skills that can help change your life for the better. Dark psychology is a well-kept secret, and by purchasing this book, you are joining a group of elite and highly skilled people from all around the world. Learning how to manipulate the people around you is an extremely valuable skill to have, and it can help you to improve your relationships with other people, advance further in your career, get more of what you want out of your life, and even feel better about yourself as a person. Soon enough, you will be an expert in the art of manipulation, and you will be able to take your destiny into your own hands like an expert manipulator.

If you have already read other books about dark psychology or have any prior knowledge about manipulation, then this book should serve nicely to supplement and improve upon what you already know. You are also likely to find out something that you did not know before somewhere within the chapters of this book, whether in the form of a manipulation technique that you were previously unaware of, an event in a case study that you had never heard of before, or something entirely different. Keep in mind that knowledge is power, and this book will help you to become an even more powerful manipulator than you already are.

No matter who you are or what your background on dark psychology and manipulation is, you will find something useful in this book. If you are more interested in the concepts that make up neuro-linguistic programming, mind control, hypnosis, and brainwashing, or you are completely new to the field of dark psychology, then I would recommend starting at the beginning and working your way through the book from there. On the other hand, if you already have knowledge of the principles of dark psychology and manipulation, or if you cannot bear the thought of theories and concepts, then the latter half of this book will be more interesting for you to read (Of course, I would still recommend going over the concepts discussed in the first few chapters before continuing on. Practice makes perfect!).

If you ever feel that you are becoming frustrated with or overwhelmed by the information contained within this book, do not be afraid to put it down and come back to it later. The following chapters contain plenty of detailed, technical information that can be difficult to absorb all at once. Frequent breaks can be incredibly useful when learning a new skill, as long as you stay determined and do not give up entirely.

Remember that manipulation techniques take time to perfect and that with enough practice; you will soon become a master of manipulation.

There are plenty of books on this subject on the market, thanks again for choosing this one! Every effort was made to ensure it is full of as much useful information as possible, please enjoy!

Chapter 1: Neuro-Linguistic Programming

Have you ever procrastinated by spending time online or bingeing television shows before completing an important project and ended up rushing to finish it in time? Or have you ever had trouble talking to people without feeling anxiety or awkwardness? Maybe you have any number of bad habits that you have been hoping to break, like biting your nails, smoking, or stress eating, but no matter how much progress you might have made in breaking them, you have never found a solution to rid yourself of these feelings or habits permanently. In that case, trying Neuro-Linguistic Programming, also referred to as NLP might work for you. NLP is made up of three components: *neuro*, which refers to the nervous system, especially in the way our brains absorb and process new information; *linguistic*, which is about analyzing language to better understand the information being conveyed in it; and *programming*, which relates back to habits, how they're formed, and how we can harness the power of the good habits and turn down the effects of the bad ones. You might be beginning to see how NLP can help you improve your life, but believe it or not, it gets even better: you can also use it to exert your influence over other people in an inconspicuous and unnoticeable way. Read on to find out more about how NLP was developed as a practice, the concepts and approaches behind NLP specialized NLP techniques, and examples of how to use NLP in the most effective, efficient way possible to improve your own life and to influence the lives of other people around you.

The History of Neuro-Linguistic Programming

The very first instance of Neuro-Linguistic Programming emerged in the United States in the 1970s as an advanced method of psychotherapy and communication, with its reported effects ranging from being able to help an average individual develop the same attributes and personality traits as successful and accomplished people to mitigating the effects of certain mental illnesses, including anxiety, depression, learning disorders, and overly intrusive phobias, as well as physical ailments such as common cold symptoms and problems with vision. NLP was developed by two men, Richard Bandler, and John Grinder, both talented self-help authors, trainers, and speakers who built the practice of NLP on the work of other professionals, including authors, psychiatrists, psychologists, anthropologists, linguists, philosophers, scholars, and psychotherapists. In 1975, Bandler and Grinder published a book called *The Structure of Magic I: A Book about Language and Therapy*, which contained the earliest concepts and abilities of the structure, uses, and effects of NLP. While neither Bandler nor Grinder was themselves trained psychiatrists, psychologists, or psychotherapists, an outside perspective may have offered them an advantage in developing NLP; Grinder stated that "My memories about what we thought at the time of discovery (with respect to the classic code we developed – that is, the years 1973 through 1978) are that we were quite explicit that we were out to overthrow a paradigm...[therefore] I believe it was very useful that neither one of us were qualified in the field we first went after – psychology and in particular, its therapeutic application." In other words, Bandler and Grinder were seeking to start a scientific revolution, and because they weren't bogged down with establishment beliefs and brought a new perspective to the discipline of psychology, they were able to accomplish precisely that.

In the late 1970s, the first workshop on NLP was held by Bandler and Grinder. It was a ten-day session attended by 150 students and covered NLP concepts and techniques to be more successful in both personal matters and business dealings. Later, Bandler and Grinder published transcripts from seminars from the workshop into a series of self-help books. Meanwhile, NLP was gaining a broader following, and a number of scientists, psychotherapists, and other professionals began to expand on and improve Bandler and Grinder's work on the practice. NLP teachings were expanded into other disciplines beyond self-improvement and business and came to be used as valuable tools in a number of different fields, such as education, leadership training, marketing, sales, parenting, therapy, and psychology. Today, over 40 years after NLP was first developed and written about, NLP has spread and blossomed into an international phenomenon, with people learning how to use its specialized techniques all over the globe. Every year, thousands of seminars train tens of thousands of people in the practice of NLP, and countless more people are exposed to the teachings of NLP through the thousands of books and guides that are currently available. And now, it's your turn to learn more about the major concepts of NLP and how to use them to your advantage.

The Key Concepts of Neuro-Linguistic Programming

As mentioned earlier, NLP can be divided into three major components, making up its name: neuro, linguistic, and programming. Of course, these are not the only concepts that govern the use and practice of NLP. In addition to neuro, linguistic, and programming, concepts such as subjectivity, consciousness, and learning (also known as modeling) are essential to the art of NLP. Having a good understanding of these concepts is the key to mastering advanced NLP techniques and procedures to be used in everyday life, as they provide a solid foundation to build and develop your NLP skills on. While the basics will be touched on in this section, more detailed techniques will be explained in the following section.

Neuro refers to the body's nervous system, in particular, the most important part of the nervous system, the brain. While human beings receive information from the outside world by using the five senses, the brain is responsible for sorting through and organizing all of the information that is received and plays a vital role in how you decide to act based on that information. Everyone's brain has a slightly different method of filtering through information: some are faster, more efficient, and more observant, while other people have to take their time in sorting information, and are not able to maximize the value they receive from it, while still others are somewhere in between the two extremes. Of course, ideally, your brain would have a filtering process that is as quick and effective as possible. By utilizing NLP techniques, you can train your brain to handle the intake of information at a faster and more productive pace, and can better determine how to use that information to gain an edge over other people in the same environment.

In NLP, your process for mentally filtering and sorting external information is crucial. After all, neuro is only the first step in the NLP process. Your first impression of the information gained from the filtering process is known as "First Access," and is comprised mainly of feelings, sounds, and images, all embedded within your subconsciousness. By being more attentive to the world around us, we can increase the strength of our First Access, and therefore have a better quality of information to feed our subconsciousness, which plays into how we make conscious decisions. Having a stronger First Access also impacts the ability to communicate with others, both on a conscious and subconscious level; if you have better access to information than another person, then you can better use that information to steer them in the direction that you want them to go.

If neuro is all about taking in outside stimuli and processing that into useable information, then *linguistic* is about what we do with that information once it has been fully sorted and processed. Once information has been gathered by the brain and has gone through First Access, we then put that information into words, both for us to be able to better understand and categorize the information as well as for us to be able to better communicate our understanding of that information in the way that best suits us and our situation. In NLP practice, the linguistic stage is known as the Linguistic Map, as well as sometimes being referred to as Linguistic Representation. While First Access is limited to the subconsciousness, the Linguistic Map is dominated by the conscious mind, which focuses on decision-making and communication skills. Therefore, having a stronger Linguistic Map will ultimately help you in developing superior decision-making and communication methods. Just like with First Access, paying more attention is the key to improving the Linguistic Map. Having a solid understanding of language and how it is used is extremely important to having a strong Linguistic Map, and by paying more attention to details such as sentence structure, speaking style, tone of voice, speaking speed, and the words being used, you can enhance the quality of information being utilized in your Linguistic Map. Having a stronger Linguistic Map also directly affects your ability to communicate with others, and if you have a better understanding of how to use language than they do, then influencing them will be much easier.

Finally, *programming* is the third step in the process and occurs after you have gathered and processed information through First Access and have conceptualized and made decisions about that information by using your Linguistic Map. Programming is critical in forming a behavioral response to information received and processed. This is where the habit-forming process comes into play: habits are built on repeating behaviors, and by having better information to build those behaviors on through a strong First Access and Linguistic Map, you can form more productive habits through stronger behavioral responses. Having a stronger sense of programming also helps you to weed out bad habits. By having a better First Access and Linguistic Map, you will no longer fuel your bad habits with poor quality information, and they will fall by the wayside as a result. Programming is also essential in manipulating the actions of other people; by having a stronger sense of behavioral responses in general, you will be able to better understand what kind of response other people will have to certain stimuli, and you can choose what information to give them in order to facilitate the reaction that you want to happen.

Of course, the concepts of neuro, linguistic, and processing are bolstered by three additional concepts: subjectivity, consciousness and learning/modeling. *Subjectivity* refers to how people perceive the world around them and the information contained within it. Rather than experiencing the world in an objective way, or based strictly on facts, human beings have a tendency to view the world from a subjective, or mainly opinionated, point of view. Because of this tendency, the information gathered from our surroundings in First Access is recorded and sorted in an inherently subjective manner. To better illustrate this point, think about the way your memory works: how often do you remember a certain event in exactly the way that it happened, with every detail preserved perfectly? You likely remember some particular parts of memory better than other parts, and even then, those parts may not even necessarily be completely correct. The way that your brain processes external information in First Access directly affects the way that you remember things, and what is memory is worthy of more importance than other parts. Fortunately, there is always a pattern in the way that subjectivity affects First Access, your Linguistic Map, and your programming and behavioral responses. By becoming more familiar with the pattern and intently studying the structure of how exactly subjectivity affects you, you can learn how to have better control over the information you take in, and from there, you can modify your behavior accordingly. Once you have a mastery over subjectivity, you can begin to directly control how subjectivity affects other people around you, allowing you to be able to shape their access to information and their behavioral responses in turn.

In addition to subjectivity, it is important to understand the concept of *consciousness*, which is divided into two separate parts: the conscious segment and the unconscious segment. The conscious segment encompasses all mental processes and behavioral responses that you have awareness and control over. On the other hand, the subconscious segment involves all actions, thoughts, and reactions that you do not have any control over. Your subconsciousness is typically associated with First Access, while your consciousness is generally correlated with the Linguistic Map; however, it is important to keep in mind that neither the subconsciousness nor the consciousness is limited solely to First Access or the Linguistic Map. All three processes contain elements of both the subconsciousness and the consciousness. For example, breathing is a subconscious behavioral response, as you do not have to actively think about breathing in order to perform the action, and it occurs largely outside of your awareness. At the same time, an example of a conscious behavioral response would be speaking, as you have to think about forming words into spoken language, and you are completely aware that you are involved in the action of speaking. In NLP, any subjective information that you gain is considered to be part of what is known as the "unconscious mind." By manipulating how subjectivity affects another person, you can influence their unconscious mind, meaning that you can program them to have specific behavioral responses to stimuli that you give them, without them ever realizing that you are actively shaping their response.

Finally, the last core concept of NLP to have a solid understanding of is *learning*, which is also commonly referred to as *modeling*. For simplicity's sake, *learning* is the term that will be used throughout the rest of this book, although you may encounter the term *modeling* elsewhere when researching NLP. Learning is widely considered to be the most difficult concept in NLP training to master, but it is also the most indispensable and necessary skill to know in order to best perform acts of manipulation and exert outside influence on the people around you. Essentially, learning is all about being able to recognize patterns in behavior and is most often used in order for ordinary people to copy the behaviors and attributes of people who are extremely talented specialists in their field, regardless of the behavior displayed by the specialists. However, once you learn how to properly utilize learning, you can also reverse engineer the concept for purposes involving manipulation. Once you understand how to analyze and imitate patterns in speech, behavior, and thought, you can better lead people to copy your own actions, and can send them down whatever path you decide on.

I know that these concepts can be difficult to comprehend at first, but by reviewing them on a regular basis, as well as seeing how they are put into practice in specific NLP techniques, you will soon come to understand them on an intimate level, and your ability to perform NLP procedures on both yourself and other people will soon become impeccable. Before we continue to the next section that will cover NLP techniques in detail, it is a good idea to take time to recap the core concepts of NLP. *Neuro* refers to the nervous system, the brain, and how the brain processes and sorts of information collected from the outside world. Neuro is covered by the NLP stage that is known as First Access. *Linguistic* refers to the way in which people use language, how the information gathered in First Access is translated into particular words and phrases, and the specific patterns and structures of communication which are used by both yourself and by everyone else around you. The NLP stage that focuses on the intricacies of linguistic is known as the Linguistic Map, or sometimes referred to as Linguistic Representation. The final NLP stage is *programming*, which refers to the behavioral response you produce to the information processed in First Access and labeled in your Linguistic Map. Tied to the three NLP stages are the concepts of subjectivity, consciousness, and learning. *Subjectivity* is the idea that information gathered from external sources is collected and sorted in a way that is based on opinion rather than fact, which then has an influence on how that information is utilized in the future. *Consciousness* refers to your awareness of thoughts, actions, and behavioral responses that occur as a result of the process of gathering and sorting information. Consciousness is divided into two different components: the subconsciousness, which has to do with all responses that you are unaware of, and the consciousness, which refers to all responses and behaviors that you have control over and actively think about. Finally, *learning*, which is also referred to as *modeling*, refers to recognizing particular patterns and specific structures in behavior and modifying your own behavior to reproduce those same behavioral patterns and structures. Read on to find out more about how the concepts of neuro, linguistic, programming, subjectivity, consciousness, and learning are combined into specific NLP techniques that can be used on anybody.

Manipulation Technique #1: In-Depth Learning Strategies

As mentioned earlier, learning is the most important component of any NLP strategy, so it is important to learn how to use it to its fullest potential in order to have a complete mastery of NLP techniques in general. Learning is essential to being able to influence others, as it allows you to get a sense of the other person and how they think, which gives you a road map that shows you the easiest way to steer them in the direction you want them to go. In order to perfect your learning methods, there are two components to learn: observation and questioning.

Observation is vital to understanding other people, especially in picking up the habits and routines of their subconsciousness. Because they are not aware of processes in their subconsciousness, they have no control over how they communicate those processes. Therefore, only by paying close attention to their movements, speaking patterns, and actions can you discern what drives their subconsciousness and how you can best influence it. Watch for physical indicators such as what they're looking at, what they're doing with their hands, how their feet are pointed, as well as linguistic elements such as word choice, sentence structure, and tone of voice. All of these subtle factors can clue you in as to how a person is thinking and feeling.

In addition to observation, questioning is essential to the learning experience. Questioning appeals more to the consciousness, although it can be useful in understanding the subconsciousness as well. Ask a person directly about themselves, and try to keep the conversation going: the longer they talk the more that you know about them, and the more time you have to observe their behavioral and linguistic habits. Be sure to ask questions asking for more detail, such as "How do you know?" and "What does that mean?" Don't be afraid to ask your target to tell you more about what they're talking about.

Once you have completed both the observation and questioning phases of learning, you can review the information you have gained by entering into a state known as "deep trance identification." First, make sure that you are sitting comfortably in a safe, secure place. Next, think about what characteristics of your target you want to most closely understand, and imagine them showing off those traits. The more time you have spent with a person, the easier this process will be. As you imagine them, let your consciousness enter their body, so that you are experiencing what they experience through sight, sound, touch, taste, and smell. This process should be a sort of meditation, and you should not by physically performing any actions; allow the target work for you. Once you feel that you have a decent understanding of the target, exit their body and return to your own. You should have retained any important information, which you can now perform yourself. Repeat the process several times, and then exit the trance. Congratulations! You now know the target's thought, speech, and behavioral patterns, which you can now reverse engineer in order to better manipulate them.

Manipulation Technique #2: Manipulating Beliefs

In many ways, beliefs are a self-fulfilling prophecy. Believing that you can do something is the first step in accomplishing it, while not believing that you can do something makes you far less likely to pursue it. By changing another person's beliefs, you can directly influence what actions they take next, or you can prevent them from taking action at all. In order to manipulate beliefs, it is crucial to understand what a belief actually is. Beliefs are made up of two parts: the body of the belief, and the significance of the belief. The body of the belief is generally a broad, sweeping statement about a certain person or thing. An example of the body of the belief is a statement such as, "My boss is not interested in what I have to say." Meanwhile, the significance of the belief encompasses the impact of the belief on your behavior. For example, the significance of the previous statement about your boss means that you likely feel resentment towards your boss, and do not work as diligently as you could as a result. By planting the body of a belief into someone's mind, including either their subconsciousness or their consciousness, the significance of the belief will take hold, and direct their future actions.

The main way to plant the body of a belief into your target's mind is through communication, which is where learning comes into play. The easiest way to initiate and follow through on successful communication strategies is to know how your target thinks and communicates themselves. They are more likely to believe something that is already familiar to them, so having some idea of what their background is or what their personality is like can pay dividends.

Of course, if you do not have access to this information, then another method of achieving familiarity is to imitate their speaking patterns. While you are planting beliefs, be sure to keep subjectivity in mind as well: because new information is processed based on opinions rather than facts, you may interpret a belief in a different way than your target. Make sure that your wording is precise, and that there is little to no chance that your statements can be misinterpreted. The more carefully you phrase a statement, the more likely that your target will internalize the body of the belief that you are attempting to implant in them.

Ideally, your wording will be exact, but also subtle; after all, if the target thinks that they developed a belief themselves, not only will they be more likely to buy into it, but it will also be virtually impossible to trace back to you. If your method of communication is not proving to be effective, do not be afraid to try a different strategy, or try again at a later time after you have completed more learning. Patience is key, and if you are not successful on your first try, do not become discouraged; with more practice and more time, you are sure to succeed. Once you have successfully implanted the body of a belief, the significance of the belief will naturally take hold in due time, and all you will have to do is simply waiting for the effects to occur.

Takeaways

As you continue on through the rest of this book, be sure to keep in mind the concepts of neuro, linguistic, programming, subjectivity, consciousness, and learning. These concepts will continue to be relevant and are critical to comprehending other topics discussed in the following chapters.

In addition, more NLP techniques will be discussed in chapters that are relevant to them. This way, these techniques can be better understood within the context of more advanced theories of dark psychology and NLP. Be sure to revisit techniques that you have already learned, and practice them often. Techniques often build on other techniques, and through frequent practice, you will be sure to hone your skills and be well on your way to becoming a master of the many uses of NLP.

Chapter 2: The Dark Triad

In order to best be able to manipulate others to the fullest extent possible, there is a commonly used and researched concept in psychology that is absolutely necessary to learn about: the Dark Triad. While the name certainly sounds sinister, it is a completely legitimate field of study within psychology, and can often be used to characterize people and behaviors in real life, even if those using it are not even aware that it exists. The Dark Triad is made up of three personality traits, which are known as narcissism, Machiavellianism, and psychopathy, all of which characterize negative social qualities in human behavior. While they all definitely sound malicious in their own way, there is nothing inherently wrong with any of the three of them. In fact, there is much that can be learned from the principles and characteristics of narcissism, Machiavellianism, and psychopathy, and by using your knowledge of the Dark Triad, you can use those principles to better influence the people around you, and you can also more easily recognize when other people are trying to use the concepts of the Dark Triad to manipulate you. While reading about the three components of the Dark Triad, be sure to keep in mind the six concepts of NLP (neuro, linguistic, programming, subjectivity, consciousness, and learning) that were discussed in the previous chapter, and try to see how they could be combined with the Dark Triad to create powerful methods of manipulation.

Concepts of the Dark Triad: Narcissism

The term narcissist is derived from an ancient Greek myth, in which a young, handsome man named Narcissus is tricked into looking at his own reflection in a river, which he falls so deeply in love with that he refuses to move and spends the rest of his life staring at himself. When you think of a narcissist, you might think of someone who displays similar behavior: someone who is obsessed about every detail of their appearance, or someone who goes out of their way to take too many selfies, or someone who generally spends far too much time being focused on themselves. But within the context of the Dark Triad, being a narcissist takes on a slightly different meaning. Narcissism is a personality trait which is characterized by a combination of pride, arrogance, pretentiousness, and most importantly, a noticeable lack of empathy. People who are narcissists are more likely to be extraverted, and they are also more likely to display signs of psychopathy as well. Men are more likely to show signs of narcissism, but a variety of studies show that the number of women who display narcissistic tendencies is generally increasing.

But what is the easiest way to recognize a narcissist? There are several telltale signs to look out for. First of all, people who are narcissists tend to have a flair for the dramatic, and view themselves as not only more important than the people around them, but also one of the most important people in the course of history overall. They tend to view themselves as better than other people, and will not treat people who they view as below their standards with empathy or consideration. In general, while most people are usually satisfied with only receiving praise as a result of a specific action or accomplishment, people who have narcissistic traits see praise as something that they are owed simply for existing. On the other hand, narcissists have a hard time dealing with even the smallest amount of criticism and are likely to be angry if ever rejected or chastised. An example of a narcissist might be a coworker who constantly complains about not being recognized for their work when they do not work as hard as they could and refuses to listen to criticism that they could be working harder. When making a determination about whether someone is a narcissist or not, you can keep the concepts of NLP in mind. For example, a narcissist's sense of subjectivity will revolve almost entirely around themselves, and they will likely either not be interested or even unable to process any information that is presented to them that does not have anything to do with themselves or their lives in general. When attempting to manipulate someone who displays narcissistic personality traits, be sure to use plenty of praise and flattery in order to make them like you more. Do not say anything that they might think is criticism or rejection, as they will be alienated by you and will likely not be open to having any future conversations with you. (Of course, if your goal is to drive away a narcissist, then be sure to stick to topics that they are not interested in, including ways that they could improve in their own lives.) Once again, using learning to its full extent will help you to influence people who are narcissists, as you will know more about them and be able to target them with more specific praise or criticisms. The more specific you are in dealing with a narcissist, the greater the chance of success you will have in achieving the outcome that you want to happen.

Concepts of the Dark Triad: Machiavellianism

Have you ever heard the phrase, "It is much safer to be feared than loved"? Or maybe the phrase, "Never attempt to win by force what can be won by deception"? Or perhaps, "Everyone sees what you appear to be; few experiences what you really are"? All of these quotes come from a book called *The Prince*, which was written by a political philosopher and strategist named Niccolo Machiavelli. Machiavelli's writings and *The Prince*, in particular, are known for advocating for ruthless, manipulative, and cynical behavior in order to get ahead in life. Similarly, people who display the trait of Machiavellianism are often extremely skilled at exploiting other people in order to influence events to go in the direction of their own self-interest. Machiavellianism goes beyond simply influencing people from time to time; people who show hallmarks of Machiavellianism are constantly thinking in a strictly strategically manner in order to fully maximize their own advantage over other people. Machiavellianism is often the most difficult attribute of the Dark Triad to recognize in others, as people who display Machiavellianism are generally secretive and are good at hiding the ways in which they manipulate other people.

Of course, there are specific signs to watch for in order to recognize whether or not Machiavellianism is present in somebody else. Most importantly, people with Machiavellian tendencies place a high priority on keeping up a public persona, which is different from who they really are. They know the value of having their peers view them in a positive light, and are careful to have their public image be as positive and harmless as possible, as that way they can better manipulate and exploit other people while avoiding the blame for any consequences that may occur as a result. For example, think of any major celebrity. They have an interest in keeping up a specific, positive public persona, so as not to drive away their fans and the fame and income that those fans provide. Some celebrities are better than this at others, and those who are involved in scandals often lose their reputation as a result, which can lead to the end of their careers. This is not to say that all celebrities have Machiavellianism as a personality trait, but by understanding the importance of having a clean public image, you can learn how to spot someone with Machiavellian tendencies much more easily. Learning is incredibly important in dealing with a person who has Machiavellian traits; by knowing as much about your target as possible, you can begin to recognize their public image, and you will know when they are using their persona and when they are exposing their true personality. Of course, maintaining a public image is not the only trait displayed by people with Machiavellianism. By paying attention to how your target treats and speaks to other people, you can determine whether or not they display Machiavellian tendencies. For instance, if your target is genuinely friendly with other people and is willing to offer their help to others, then they most likely do not possess Machiavellianism as a personality trait. However, if they take other people help more often than offer their own and treat people as tools to accomplish their own goals rather than friends, and then the target most likely has Machiavellian tendencies. These differences can be difficult to pick up on, but if you pay enough attention, eventually you will notice a pattern in your target's behavior.

When attempting to manipulate a person with Machiavellian tendencies by using NLP techniques, you must be sure to be extremely careful. After all, they are incredibly skilled manipulators themselves, and will not have a difficult time picking up on what you are attempting to do if you are not precise. The best way to try to influence people who display Machiavellianism is to appeal to their sense of self-interest. If you put them in a situation that directly benefits them, then even if they know that you are trying to manipulate them, they will still go along with you, as they know that they will ultimately gain something. Of course, if what you are trying to influence them to do might be harmful to them, then appealing to their sense of self-interest will not work. Instead, you can threaten to expose their private life and reveal the truth about their public image. Privacy is incredibly important to people who display Machiavellianism, so if you can manage to threaten their privacy, they will go to extreme measures to protect it. When dealing with a person with Machiavellian tendencies, you have to be sure to be subtle. Hide your intentions in carefully precise language, and never explicitly reveal anything about your plans for what you want them to do. After all, if you tell them anything directly, not only will they know that you are attempting to influence them, but they will also try to manipulate you in response. It is extremely difficult to out-manipulate someone who displays Machiavellianism, so it is best to avoid those battles completely if you are able to.

Concepts of the Dark Triad: Psychopathy

When you think of a psychopath, you most likely think of someone who is a cold, unfeeling, violent criminal, or someone who gets enjoyment out of doing horrible things to other people. While psychopathy is largely considered to be the most dangerous trait out of the Dark Triad, its actual characteristics are a little bit different from those displayed by popular stereotypes of psychopaths. In real life, psychopaths tend to seek out thrills, show poor levels of impulse control and have a distinct lack of empathy for other people. They also tend to display antisocial behavior, and studies have shown that there is a link between psychopathy and antisocial personality disorder. Of course, this does not mean that most psychopaths simply shut themselves away from the rest of the world; instead, they have lots of difficulty with forming lasting, healthy relationships with other people, and have no problem with ruining another person's life on a whim. In general, try not to think of psychopaths as terrifying, emotionless serial killers, and think of them more as an attractive, charismatic wolf in sheep's clothing who are skilled at charming people into relationships that turn out to be disastrous for the victim. People with psychopathic tendencies are more common than you might think and include a high proportion of CEOs, major executives, billionaires, and other extremely successful people. This is because their remorselessness and their nearly complete lack of empathy allow them to make difficult, ruthless decisions that other people might morally struggle with, and so they are able to gain an advantage in their field and achieve massive levels of success.

Because psychopaths are so dangerous to form relationships with, it can be very difficult to be able to identify someone as a psychopath while still remaining safe. Psychopaths do fit better into certain groups of people than others; for example, men are far more likely to display psychopathic traits than women, and certain research has indicated that blacks, Native Americans, and Hispanics are more likely to have psychopathic tendencies than whites and Asians. Of course, keep in mind that these patterns are not in any way definitive proof that someone is or is not a psychopath, and that anybody can have psychopathic personality traits. One other way to more easily determine whether or not someone is a psychopath is by first identifying them as either a narcissist or as someone with Machiavellian tendencies. Research has shown that both narcissism and Machiavellianism have a positive correlation with psychopathy, meaning that if someone is a narcissist or has Machiavellian personality traits, then there is a greater chance that they might also be a psychopath. This works both ways: if you identify someone as a psychopath, then there are also significantly likely to show signs of narcissism, Machiavellianism, or both. This is in part why psychopaths are such dangerous individuals; by having a combination of more than one component of the Dark Triad, they show high skill levels of manipulative behavior and lack any ethical concerns about how they use those skills on the people around them. Everything that they do is done to exclusively benefit themselves or to directly harm other people. Therefore, it is very important that you do not fall for a psychopath's charms because if you do, your life will likely be ruined by the psychopath in a matter of time.

Because of the danger that psychopaths pose to your safety, attempting to use learning techniques to fully understand them is not always a good option. When you observe a person with psychopathic tendencies from a distance, however, you will have a better chance of identifying them while keeping any risk to your own safety at an absolute minimum. With this in mind, in addition to the common physical characteristics that many psychopaths have and the overlapping personality traits of the Dark Triad that they might possess, there are also certain patterns in behavior and methods of speaking to look out for. One of the most major traits that psychopaths commonly possess is certain attractiveness to other people. While psychopaths can certainly be physically attractive, and many of them are, this attractiveness is more in line with a general charisma. Psychopaths excel at luring in other people by using an engaging personality, and their victims are drawn to them like magnets. Of course, there is a difference between someone having the charisma that is natural and someone that is charming because they have manufactured a charming personality. Psychopaths do not actually care about the people who are drawn to them and the charm that a psychopath display is never deeper than surface level. People with psychopathic tendencies will never use more charisma than is absolutely necessary to lure in their victims. When trying to determine whether or not someone is a psychopath, trust your gut instinct; if something does not feel genuine, then it most likely is not, and you are probably being manipulated.

Another recurring trait to look out for when attempting to identify psychopathic traits is dishonesty. Psychopaths are notorious, habitual liars, and will display dishonesty about anything from even the smallest details to the largest, most consequential pieces of information. If you manage to catch someone in multiple lies, regardless of whether or not they are told to you or to another person, then there is a good chance that that person displays psychopathic tendencies. If you think that someone might be a psychopath, be sure to be a skeptic of anything that that person tells you, and use your best judgment. Of course, not all liars have psychopathic tendencies, and accusing someone of being a psychopath is a good way to drive them away permanently. Because of this, if you catch your target in a series of multiple lies, do not immediately assume that they are a psychopath and do not accuse them of anything. Instead, either confront them about their lies or wait for someone else to do so, and take note of their reaction: do they regret having to lie, or do they seem unworried about it? Remember that people with psychopathic tendencies generally to not feel guilt or remorse for their actions, so a person who sincerely regrets lying is probably not a psychopath. It is important to keep in mind that having a good excuse for lying is not the same thing as expressing guilt, so even if your target has a legitimate excuse for telling lies, if they do not hold any regrets about the incident, then they still could very well be a psychopath.

Manipulating a person who displays psychopathic tendencies may seem impossible, but if you are sure to hone your skills to the level of an expert and exercise the utmost caution, it can be done. Once you learn how to recognize their methods of using charm and charisma to lure in their victims, you will also know how to avoid these same methods. That way, you can get close to someone that you suspect is a psychopath and begin to use learning to model their personality traits without being at risk of danger or harm to yourself. By recognizing a psychopath's attempts at using a fabricated, charismatic personality, you can pretend to be drawn in, but you will not be tempted to make any decisions that might end up presenting very serious harm to your health. In fact, if you are good enough at playing along with a psychopath, then you are at an advantage. If you do not allow them to realize that you are simply pretending to be drawn to their personality, then they are far more likely to underestimate you and not see you as a threat to themselves. Once you have fooled the psychopath, you can use NLP techniques as you would any other person. Because psychopaths are often more impulsive than the average person and actively seek out thrills, they might also follow your suggestions more readily than other people, especially if you make your suggestions sound exciting and interesting. When attempting to influence anyone with psychopathic tendencies, of course, caution is the most important thing to remember. If at any point you do not feel safe while using NLP techniques on a psychopath be sure to walk away and choose a new target before you end up in real trouble. After all, once you have practiced your skills more, you can always come back to your target at a later time.

Why Should You Care About The Dark Triad?

At this point in the chapter, you may be wondering why the Dark Triad is covered at all in the book. After all, people who display narcissistic, Machiavellianism, psychopathy, or a combination of all three are generally rare. However, there are important lessons to be learned from the three concepts that form the Dark Triad. Now that you know what the hallmarks of the Dark Triad are and how to recognize them in other people, you can use those same hallmarks to your advantage. You see, none of the three traits in the Dark Triad are explicitly harmful unless used to an extreme degree. People do not have to be narcissists, Machiavellian, or psychopaths in order to display behavior that is commonly associated with those traits. The average person uses many of the tactics belonging to the Dark Triad every day, often without even realizing that they are doing it. At some point in your life, you have also used these same tactics to get ahead and achieve success. Therefore, there is no harm in integrating the features of narcissism, Machiavellianism, and psychopathy in with your NLP techniques. Using the principles of the Dark Triad can help you be more flexible in using NLP techniques and can help you find more success in influencing people to do what you want them to do. You might have noticed already that all three components of the Dark Triad involve the skilled use of manipulation, and you can see how imitating narcissism, Machiavellianism, and psychopathy might be useful to you in pursuing the art of manipulation.

Narcissism, for example, teaches you that other people tend to prefer praise over criticism, and by appealing to their sense of self-worth, you will have a much easier time in convincing your target to go along with what you want for them to do. In a similar vein of thought, Machiavellianism teaches you that by thinking about other people in purely strategic terms and by valuing your own needs above the needs of other people, you will maximize the benefit that other people give you and you will better be able to position them in places that you want them to be in. While extremely dangerous, psychopathy teaches you to use your personality to its full extent as a resource in manipulating other people and to not be afraid to cut off relationships with others when the timing best suits you. While you should not practice any of the values of narcissism, Machiavellianism, and psychopathy to a harmful extent, do not be afraid to integrate them into your NLP techniques, as they will make you better and more effective at influencing the people around you.

The Dark Triad: Recap

I know that this chapter covered a lot of information, so it's important to take a moment to review everything. These concepts of the Dark Triad will continue to be relevant throughout the rest of this book, so it is vital to know them well. First of all, the Dark Triad is a well-studied and researched topic in contemporary psychology, and is made up of three distinct components, which are known as narcissism, Machiavellianism, and psychopathy. Narcissism is named after Narcissus, the character from ancient Greek mythology, and is characterized by self-obsession, a need for praise, an overbearing sense of superiority to other people, and a lack of empathy for other people.

The second component of the Dark Triad is Machiavellianism, which is named for the political philosopher Niccolo Machiavelli, and encompasses personality traits such as valuing one's own self-interest at the expense of other people, being ruthless and uncompromising, having a separate public persona from one's own self, and a desire for privacy at all times. Psychopathy is the most dangerous concept in the Dark Triad and is characterized by being impulsive and seeking thrills, displaying antisocial behavior, and using charisma and charm to reel in potential victims before ruining their lives. When attempting to manipulate anyone with explicit personality traits belonging to the Dark Triad, in particular when dealing with people who might be psychopaths, be sure to be careful, and never put yourself in a situation that might be harmful or dangerous. Being able to recognize narcissism, Machiavellianism, and psychopathy in other people is a useful skill, although it can be more difficult to manipulate people who possess one or more of the traits contained within the Dark Triad. Of course, once you know enough about narcissism, Machiavellianism, and psychopathy, you can begin to integrate them into your own NLP techniques to become even more skilled at influencing the people around you, just as long as you are sure to be cautious and not take the three traits to the extreme. As Machiavelli stated in *The Prince*, "He who seeks to deceive will always find someone who will allow himself to be deceived."

As you continue to make your way through the rest of this book, be sure to keep the concepts of narcissism, Machiavellianism, and psychopathy in mind. You should try to apply them to future concepts and techniques that will be discussed, as the concepts contained within the Dark Triad will often enrich NLP tactics and make them even more effective to use.

Chapter 3: Persuasion and Deception

So far in this book, the term "manipulation" has been brought up over and over again. But what does manipulation really mean, and how does it actually work? While both the six core concepts of NLP and the three traits that make up the Dark Triad certainly make up a part of the puzzle of manipulation, there are two other concepts that are also incredibly important to know about: persuasion and deception. While these two concepts may seem like the same thing, they are actually two separate entities, and should not be confused with each other. Think of that difference like this: persuasion is all about trying to get another person to believe in what you are saying, while deception is more about trying to get another person to believe that *you* believe in what you are saying. While they are similar, they both have different strategies in order to use them effectively, and they both relate back to the concepts of NLP and the Dark Triad in different ways. A master of manipulation should know the difference between persuasion and deception, and how to use both of these concepts by utilizing their respective strategies and tactics to their full effect. Once you are familiar with persuasion and deception, the principles of most NLP techniques, as well as more advanced manipulation procedures such as mind control, hypnosis, and brainwashing, should come much more easily to you and feel more natural to use.

Psychology, Robert Cialdini, and the Six Principles of Persuasion

Persuasion is well-studied in the world of psychology, and there are many guides, books, and websites dedicated to the subject. One of the most famous and respected books are called *Influence: The Psychology of Persuasion*, written by a man named Robert Cialdini. Cialdini is an accomplished psychologist, college professor, author, and public speaker, and is known as the "guru of social influence."

In his book, he outlined six separate principles that make up the art of persuasion, which he discovered from his time spent studying car dealerships, telemarketing phone banks, and organizations that work to raise massive amounts of money and the training programs that they use to prepare new employees for their jobs. The six principles of persuasion that Cialdini identified are as follows: authority, reciprocity, likeability, commitment and consistency, social proof, and scarcity. In 2016, he discovered another principle of persuasion, which he referred to as the unity principle. For simplicity's sake, this chapter will only be covering the original six principles of persuasion, and will not include the unity principle, as it shares many characteristics with the other six principles. By learning more about authority, reciprocity, likeability, commitment and consistency, social proof, and scarcity, and by combining these principles with the six concepts of NLP and the three components of the Dark Triad, you will have a very thorough background in the art of influencing and manipulating other people, and you will be ready to move on to the more advanced and more difficult concepts of mind control, hypnosis, and brainwashing, and you will be well-prepared to use these concepts in the real world rather than just in theory.

The Six Principles of Persuasion: Authority

You are probably familiar with the commonly used cliché that in commercials that advertise toothpaste, something similar to the phrase "Four out of five dentists recommend this brand" at some point in the advertisement. This is because the marketing team behind these commercials has a good understanding of the principle of authority, which simply states that human beings are more likely to believe other people who appear as if they know what they are doing. I have already used the principle of authority in this very chapter when I mentioned Robert Cialdini and his many accomplishments and credentials. Of course, while having and talking about accomplishments and credentials is certainly useful when attempting to establish your authority, it is not necessarily a requirement to have those things. Go back and read the definition of the principle of authority one more time. The keyword to keep in mind is "appear." You do not have to actually know what you are talking about or be an established expert in your field so long as you can convince people that you know what you are talking about. As long as you do some research ahead of time or manage to come up with terms and phrases that seem to be legitimate, then you can easily fool another person into believing that you know more about that field than they do and that they should listen to what you are saying. Confidence is key, and if you can convince yourself that you are correct in what you are saying, it will be far easier to convince other people as well. It is also useful to keep in mind that in general, people are more likely to believe people who claim to be experts in fields that they are not already familiar with. This makes sense: it would be much more difficult, if not impossible, to convince someone who is already an expert in their chosen field of something in that field that they have not heard of before. Therefore, when selecting a target to use the principle of authority on, be sure to find out whether they already have some background knowledge of a topic or not before you try to convince them of something.

In addition to these baseline rules in the principle of authority, there are also other tricks that you can use if you really want to convince someone that you know what you are talking about. In addition to simply being confident and talking about a subject as if you know all about it already, there are other visual cues that people pick up on in order to determine whether somebody is an expert or not. The first visual cue that you can use is wearing a uniform. Costumes are handy for more than just Halloween; by wearing a uniform, you have become visually associated with the topic that you are pretending to be an expert in, which will add to your overall believability. Think about it like this: would you be more open to believing that someone is a pilot if they were wearing an old t-shirt and ratty jeans, or would you believe them more if they were in their full uniform? Of course, uniforms are not completely foolproof, and they can be expensive and time-consuming to obtain or create. Fortunately, there are other cues that you can use in order to better convince people of your authority. The uses of specific titles that are associated with a particular field are also highly useful when you are using the principle of authority. For example, a title such as "Dr." lets you know that the person in question has earned a doctorate degree, and has a huge amount of knowledge about a specific topic. Titles can also include specific jobs. For instance, if someone tells you that they are an attorney, then you would be more inclined to believe that they know about the law and legal processes more than someone who is not an attorney. Linking a job title to a specific company and being able to explain what the job involves is also helpful when you are attempting to establish authority.

The Six Principles of Persuasion: Reciprocity

The principle of reciprocity is, at its core, very simple: people are going to be more likely to follow your lead if they feel that they owe you something. If you can make someone feel indebted to you, then they will be motivated to pay back that debt in whatever way they can, including by being convinced to do something that they would not normally do. Of course, there are a few tricks to getting reciprocity to work for you in the right way. Just because you give somebody else something random does not mean that they will feel that they owe you anything. Reciprocity works best when it is used in a selective, strategic way, so you have to think it through in a thorough way in order to have it be as effective as possible for you. There are three components that you can use in order to make the principle of reciprocity work well: be the first one to offer something, make your offer unique, and make sure that your offer can only come from you. By following these three steps, the person who receives your offer will understand that you have taken the time to consider all of their needs, and will, therefore, have a greater likelihood of feeling like they need to pay you back for your gift.

The first component in performing the principle of reciprocity is perhaps the most important out of all of them. When you make sure that you are the first one to offer your target something, you are laying the foundation for their feelings of gratitude and obligation to you. Do not allow them to offer something to you first, as in that case, you are the one who much pay them back, which do not benefit you. In a similar vein, do not stand by and let another person offer your target something before you can do so. You will be giving up your relationship with your target to another person, and they will become indebted to that person, not to you. This first component requires patience from you; you have to make your offer at the right time, in order to maximize the other person's feelings of obligation towards you. If you make your offer at the wrong time, then the other two components in the principle of reciprocity will no longer be of any use to you, and you will have to try another tactic or technique on your target.

Along with being the first person to make an offer to your target, you have to also make sure that your offer is unique to them. If you offer your target something that you could have offered to anybody, then your offer will not be as effective. By specifically personalizing your offer to your target's own personality, you will make them feel special, and because of that the level of gratitude they will fell towards you will be much higher than normal, and they will be more likely to do what you want them to do. The more you make your offer unique to your target, the more likely that person will be willing to do things that they would normally be uncomfortable with doing. If being the first one to offer your target something will first make them feel that they owe you something, then making your offer unique to them will make them less likely to say no to whatever it is you want for them to do, no matter what it is.

The third concept in the principle of reciprocity, being sure that your offer can only come from you, is very similar to the second concept. If anybody can offer what you are offering, after all, why should your target feel particularly indebted to you? You need to work hard to set yourself apart from the rest of the pack, or else your target will not be willing to follow your lead. You can see how this concept ties in neatly with the other two: by being the first person to make an offer, making sure that that offer is personalized to the person that you are trying to manipulate, and being careful to make sure that your offer can only come from you, you offer will be very compelling to your target, and it is incredibly unlikely that they will turn it down. Once they have accepted your offer, let their feelings of gratitude sink in for a couple of days, and then make a suggestion of what you want your target to do for you. Instead of being demanding, try to use a friendly tone, and only remind them that they owe you if they explicitly refuse to do what you want them to. The more aggressive you are, the less they will want to work with you any longer, and their feelings of obligation to you will not be enough to keep them involved with you if you drive them away.

The Six Principles of Persuasion: Likeability

Likeability is perhaps the easiest of the six principles to understand and to perfect, as you likely already deal with likeability on a regular basis in your own life. The principle of likeability simply states that human beings are more likely to go along with suggestions from people who they like. This means that someone who is your friend is going to be easier for you to influence, but the principle of likeability is not limited only to friends. For example, if your favorite celebrity endorses a certain product, then you will likely view that product in a more favorable light and will be more likely to buy it, even though you do not personally know the celebrity. Therefore, you will be more successful in using the principle of likeability if you are able to form a relationship with your target, whether genuine or not. There are a couple of tricks that can help you be more successful with likeability. First of all, people who you do not already know will be more likely to want to be your friend if you are more physically attractive, so taking care of your appearance is important when attempting to use likeability. Of course, being physically attractive is not a requirement for likeability to work; in fact, since what each individual finds attractive is different from person to person, physical attractiveness is highly subjective, and may only help you out in certain situations. Another tip that you can keep in mind is to use compliments to your advantage. When you first meet somebody else, try to pick something out from their appearance to compliment; it can be something that they are wearing, such as a shirt or jewelry, or a physical attribute, like their eyes or their hair. Everyone likes to feel good about themselves, and compliments can be an easy way to fulfill that need. After you have started to get to know your target a little bit better, there are additional strategies in the principle of likeability that you can use. For example, be sure to keep in touch with your target. Modern technology has made it easier than ever to stay in contact with people, and while you should not harass your target or try to talk to them too much, you should not let them forget that you are there, either. If you can, try to see them in person on a regular basis. If they invite you to go somewhere, do not turn them down. The more you stay in contact with your target, especially when you are consistently meeting them face-to-face, the closer they will feel to you, and the more open they will be to doing whatever you suggest. Even if you cannot form a close friendship with whoever your target it, try to make contact with them before you attempt to influence them so they have at least a little bit of familiarity with who you are.

The Six Principles of Persuasion: Commitment and Consistency

To best understand the principle of commitment and consistency, take a moment to think about a river. Rivers flow in one, singular path, and it is often very difficult to force a river to follow a **different** path. In many ways, human beings behave in a similar manner. Once a person has committed to a specific plan of action or a certain set of beliefs, they will be consistent in following through on that plan or those beliefs, and it can be difficult to try to make somebody else change their mind. While this might seem like it would make it hard to manipulate someone into doing something they do not want to do, you can easily make the principle of commitment and consistency work for you. Using commitment and consistency is all about establishing a pattern with your target. If you know enough about them that you can piggyback off of an existing set of beliefs, then doing so will make manipulating them much easier. However, if what you are trying to influence your target to do go against their established set of beliefs, then you can still work around that. In that case, you should try to create a new pattern for your target to follow. Start with small things and work your way up to larger tasks, as this will allow for them to become ingrained in a new set of habits, and will make them more open to doing whatever you suggest. When trying to influence a target while using commitment and consistency, be sure to reward your target for following your lead. When you give them positive reinforcement, their idea of commitment to you and your influences will be more positive overall, and they will be more likely to go along with whatever you want in the future. The principle of commitment and consistency works best when it is combined with one of the other six principles of persuasion; for example, it works well with the principle of likeability. With likeability, if you have a strong relationship with your target already, then you have created a path for them to follow, and by force of habit, they will be more likely to do whatever it is that you want for them to do. Remember, with commitment and consistency, your first attempt at influencing your target will always be the hardest. So long as you implant a pattern of behavior into your target's mind, they will be easier to influence in your future attempts.

The Six Principles of Persuasion: Social Proof

Social proof is very similar to the principles of authority and likeability but occupies a slightly different set of ideas. Essentially, the principle of social proof holds that people tend to go along with whatever is already popular or whatever has already been recommended by people who are popular. The second part of the principle of social proof includes a wide range of people, including professionals or experts in a given field, famous people, and groups of people, which is also referred to as the "wisdom of crowds." This is why the vast majority of online stores have space where reviews can be left on a particular product; even though other customers on the website are anonymous to you, when you see a large group of positive reviews, you are more likely to consider buying that product. But how do you apply the principle of social proof to manipulate other people? There are a couple of different methods that you can try to use. First of all, you can do some research before beginning to try to influence your target. If you can find quotes, books, or other works from a well-known person or from a large group of other people, your own reasoning behind your influences will seem to be much more solid, and your target will have a harder time in seeing any flaws or leaps of logic in your arguments. The more sources that you have to back you up, the more credible you seem, and the less your target will be able to rationalize away why they might not want to be influenced by you. The other method that you can use to get used out of the principle of social proof is to team up with another person or even a group of several people in order to influence your target. You on your own are not a crowd, but if you can find people with similar goals and desires to your own, you can create your own crowd. Once your target finds themselves surrounded by people with the same mindset as you, they will have little choice but to go along with you. Of course, you have to be careful when creating your own group, as you do not want to frighten your target away or make them feel intimidated. Keep your group small, and try to prevent them from getting aggressive. It is also important to be sure that all members of your group are loyal to you and that you retain control of the group, as you do not want to worry about anyone in the group telling your target what you are attempting to do to them.

The Six Principles of Persuasion: Scarcity

The principle of scarcity is a bit different from the other six principles. Scarcity is the idea that if something is rare, limited in quantity, or hard to come by, people will be more drawn to it and want to have it more than something that is commonly available. To better illustrate the concept of scarcity, imagine yourself in a room with eight other people, and all of you are hungry. Now imagine that a pizza is delivered, and there is just enough of it for everybody to be able to have a slice. All eight people in the room are now satisfied because they each got a slice of pizza. Now, imagine the same situation, but instead of there being eight slices available, there is only one slice. The singular slice in the second situation has a far greater value than the eight slices in the first situation since not everybody will be able to be fed. This is the principle of scarcity in action. Scarcity can be valuable to keep in mind when attempting to manipulate another person because of the effect it has on a person's decision-making habits. For example, when a company advertises a product as a limited edition version, they are creating scarcity in order to encourage its customers to buy it, a strategy that works most of the time. If people are afraid that they might miss out on something, they will be more likely to try to obtain it while not taking into consideration any negative consequences. Limited edition versions of a product are more expensive for a reason; the product's scarcity is more important to consumers than its price is. You can use the principle of scarcity in your own attempts to manipulate the people around you. If a person feels that they could do whatever you want them to do at any time, then they will not feel as urgent about listening to you. However, if you frame whatever you want your target to do as a limited-time opportunity that they could potentially miss out on, then your target will feel more motivated to do what you want them to do. When you are attempting to use the principle of scarcity, remember that it is more important to be a salesperson than a manipulator. The more you sell what you want your target to do, the more likely your target is to be invested in that action, and the more that they will feel that they would be missing out on something if they do not follow your instructions.

Deception

Remember, deception is a slightly different concept than persuasion, and while it has not been studied to the same extent as persuasion, it can be just as useful in your manipulation attempts. Deception can range between a wide variety of uses, from small lies to enormous scams. While deception is generally considered to be more malevolent than persuasion, there is nothing inherently wrong with either of them and in fact, people use tactics that are associated with both of them on a regular basis. In fact, the six principles of persuasion can easily be blended with tactics used in deception to make you an even better manipulator.

But what are some deceptive tactics? The first and most important tactic is the art of lying. Lying is the most commonly used tool of manipulation, and is used all the time by people all around the world. Everyone has lied at some point in their lives, but of course, some people are better at it than others. The most skilled liars know that lying is most effective when it is used along with the truth. Not only does mixing the truth and lies together help you remember what you said, but it also makes it easier for your target to believe what you are saying. Lies are also more convincing when your target is not familiar with the thing that you are lying about. A person is not likely to question information when they do not know about any alternatives, but when they have some idea of what the truth actually is, then you will need to work hard to convince them that their information is faulty.

Another tactic of deception that is easy to use is the act of omission. Omission simply means that you are telling the truth, but not all of it. The omission is easier to use than lying is, but it cannot always be used as a tactic in any situation. Oftentimes, it is best to use omission in addition to lying, or as an excuse to fall back on if you are ever caught in a lie. If your target believes that you are lying about a certain subject, then your best strategy is to abandon the subject entirely and move on to a new one. For example, when speaking about a particular topic, you can always change the flow of the conversation by saying that you forgot the rest of whatever story you were telling, and move on to a new topic of discussion. You can also say that you were traumatized by a certain event, which gives you a good excuse not to talk about it any further and move on to a new topic.

Takeaways

Along with the six concepts of NLP and the three personality traits that make up the Dark Triad, the principles of persuasion and deception are the final pieces of the puzzle that makes up mind control, hypnosis, and brainwashing techniques. By having a good understanding of all of these concepts, you should be able to easily pick up and eventually master everything presented to you in the following chapters. However, you should return to these first three chapters frequently and review what you have learned so far. After all, without being able to sufficiently understand the basics, you will have a more difficult time being able to perfect anything that is more advanced. Also, keep in mind the old mantra that practice makes perfect, and the more time that you spend practicing these basic concepts, the more naturally that mind control, hypnosis, and brainwashing will come to you. Above all else, never feel discouraged, and remember that setbacks are a part of the learning experience. If you ever feel stuck, just return to these earlier chapters and try to gain a new perspective on the concepts covered within them.

Chapter 4: Mind Control

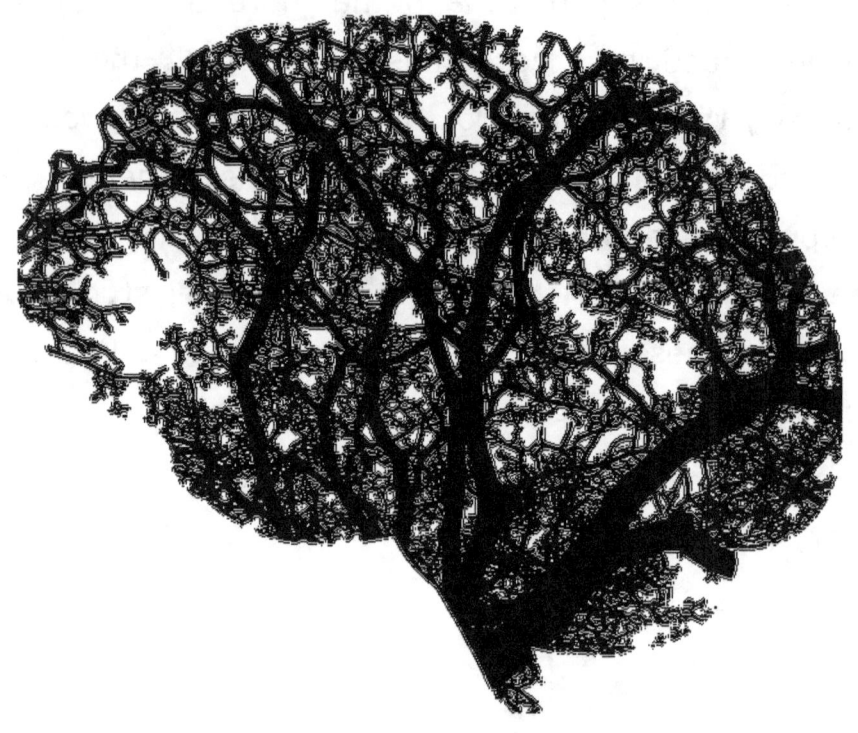

Now that you know all about the concepts of NLP, the three components that make up the Dark Triad, and the principles of persuasion and deception, you are finally ready to move on to the concepts and techniques that make up mind control, hypnosis, and brainwashing. But of course, you may be wondering what the difference between mind control, hypnosis, and brainwashing are and what separates those three concepts from simple manipulation and influencing.

This chapter will cover those differences in detail, as well as debunking popular myths about how mind control actually works and teaching you techniques that are proven to be effective. This chapter will also work to relate all new concepts back to the foundation that has already been laid by the concepts of NLP, the Dark Triad, and the principles of persuasion and deception. Keep reading to master the techniques of mind control so that you can become an even better manipulator!

What Is The Difference Between Mind Control, Hypnosis, And Brainwashing?

Mind control, hypnosis, and brainwashing are all closely linked together as concepts, but it is important to keep in mind their differences so that you know which one is the best technique to use in whatever situation you might find yourself in. Keep in mind that hypnosis and brainwashing will be discussed in detail in the next two chapters, and this section is not meant to explain them to their fullest potential. This section is only meant to distinguish hypnosis and brainwashing from the concept of mind control. While all three terms have to do with extreme, powerful manipulation techniques, they all work in slightly different ways, and you might find that one works better for you than the other two. They all have both pros and cons in their use, and if you want to become a master of manipulation, you should have a good understanding of all three concepts.

Mind control is perhaps the most subtle out of the three concepts, but it is also easily the broadest as well. Mind control refers to any series of words, actions, or behaviors that you can speak or perform in order to take command of another person's mental processes and dominate them. Ideally, when you perform mind control techniques, your target should not be aware of what you are doing, both before they have been mind-controlled and afterward. Your target should not be able to trace mind control back to you. Instead, you should be able to use mind control techniques without being detected, which is made easier when you model your mind control techniques on concepts from NLP, the Dark Triad, and the principles of persuasion and deception. In addition, mind control is not a permanent procedure. While you can certainly perform mind control techniques on a particular target more than once, they will not remain mind-controlled by you for a very long time. There are ways to extend the amount of time that your target is mind-controlled, but they will never remain mind-controlled for incredibly long periods of time. Out of the three concepts, mind control is the easiest to pull off successfully and requires the fewest amounts of resources for you to use.

Hypnosis is easiest to think of as the middle ground between mind control and brainwashing. You can perform hypnosis in either a subtle or a more involved way, which is why hypnosis is the most flexible of the three concepts. You see, hypnotic suggestions can be made in one of two different ways: verbal or nonverbal. Verbal hypnotic techniques are just what they sound like: they involve using language in a very specific way in order to hypnotize your target. On the other hand, nonverbal hypnotic techniques are performed through specialized behaviors and actions. (Both verbal and nonverbal hypnotic techniques will be discussed in more detail in Chapter 5.) Just like with mind control, hypnosis is very difficult for a target to successfully detect, and should not be traceable back to you. However, unlike mind control, hypnosis cannot be performed on just anybody, so you must be careful to choose your targets with care. Overall, hypnosis is the concept that relates the most easily back to the concepts of NLP and is more powerful and has an effect that lasts longer than mind control, but it requires more knowledge, more skill, and more precise target selection to pull off than mind control does, so it cannot be used in as many situations as mind control can be. However, if you have enough practice with it, then hypnosis can be invaluable in manipulating people to do what you want without them ever knowing about it.

Out of all three concepts, brainwashing takes the longest amount of time to pull off, but it is also by far the longest-lasting and most effective method of them all. Brainwashing requires more skill, patience, and discipline to use than mind control and hypnosis, but it will also more deeply affect your targets for a longer duration of time than the other two concepts. Like hypnosis, brainwashing is most effective only on certain people, and may not work on everybody that you try it on, so you have to be sure to choose your targets carefully and strategically. Similarly to both mind control and hypnosis, if performed correctly, brainwashing should be undetectable by your target, and they should not be able to trace it back to you once the process has been completed. However, brainwashing has an additional component that both mind control and hypnosis lack: even if it was possible for your target to be able to trace brainwashing techniques back to you if you are precise in how you perform brainwashing techniques, then they would not even want to attempt to trace it back to you. (Brainwashing techniques will be discussed in more detail in Chapter 6.) While brainwashing is by far the most powerful of the three concepts, it is also extremely time-consuming and difficult to pull off correctly, so it is not always the most ideal method to use unless you have unlimited time and plenty of skill to dedicate to your target.

Mind Control: Myths vs. Reality

Take a moment to think about how mind control is portrayed in movies, books, and the media. What popular stereotypes and commonly used tropes come to mind? You might have thought of someone with superpowers, taking complete control of another person just by touching their fingers to the side of their head. Or you might have thought of a situation in which someone's entire reality is all part of a giant, elaborate simulation, which causes them to think and act in very specific ways. Of course, no matter what example you thought of, chances are very good that it did not show what mind control is or how it works in a completely correct manner. But there is a reason why so many stories involving the use of mind control are so compelling; as the author Terry O'Brian stated, "Mind control is such a powerful image that if hypnotism did not exist, then something similar would have to have been invented: the plot device is too useful for any writer to ignore. The fear of mind control is equally as powerful an image." While he mistakenly uses the word "hypnotism" in place of mind control, his statement has plenty of truth and wisdom to follow, especially the last part. To most people, their mind is a sacred place and something that only they ever have access to, and having their control over their mind is taken away by something or somebody else is a terrifying thought to have. In fact, it is such a terrifying thought that it is also seen as an outlandish or even impossible task to pull off, and is portrayed in movies, books, and other media in a ridiculous and over-the-top way. What these stories do not confront, however, is that mind control is a subtle, gentle process, and is not nearly as powerful as it is portrayed to be.

While it can be fun to look at the ways in which mind control is presented to an everyday audience and point out all of its flaws and the ways in which it is completely wrong, there is also a valuable lesson to be learned from these stories. Most crucially, these portrayals give newcomers a good idea of what mind control specifically is not, which is important in order for you to temper your expectations. If you are expecting mind control to work in the same way that it does in movies when you are first beginning to practice it, you will become disappointed and may lose interest in pursuing mind control and manipulation, in general, any further. By having more realistic expectations of what mind control is and what it is capable of, however, you can avoid being disappointed and you can be more confident in your abilities, which is critical if you ever want to become a master of manipulation. In addition, the way that mind control is portrayed in popular media can also be useful to you as an excuse to fall back on. The fact that the power and use of mind control are so ludicrous in stories actually provides you an advantage, as most people do not believe that mind control really works or exists at all. This is good for you for a number of reasons. First of all, because your target is not aware that the mind control methods that you are using actually exist, they will be much less likely to notice that you are doing anything to them at all. Secondly, if you are ever accused of using mind control techniques on another person, whether by your target or by a different person, then you have an excuse to fall back on. You can easily claim that because you are not performing any actions that might be shown in a movie as valid mind control techniques, then you cannot possibly be mind-controlling your target. In fact, you can also say that you think that mind control is ridiculous and you do not believe that it is actually real, which is a reasonable thing to say within the context of how mind control is portrayed in books and movies. You can even use a particular book or movie as an example, which is likely to make your accuser feel embarrassed and not want to press the issue any further. As long as you are willing to be creative and do not mind employing some of the principles of deception, you can easily turn around the way in which mind control is portrayed to work in popular stories and make it work for you in ways that might not be expected.

Manipulation Technique #3: Mind Control, Storytelling, and Controlling the Narrative

At its very core, mind control is all about the flow of information. The better you control how information is used and what information is given to your target, the more control you will ultimately have over their mind and their actions. This is why the way that you choose to present information to your target is extremely important. In order to best control the way in which you introduce new information to your target, it is vital to understand the technique of how to control the narrative. Think of controlling the narrative like telling a story: the more relatable, engaging, and well-told your story is, the more likely your target is to feel a connection with it and believe in it. Controlling the narrative is a useful tool because it allows for you to easily implant new beliefs in another person's mind, and if those beliefs are expressed in a compelling way, then they are much more likely to stick around for a much longer, extended period of time.

But what are the best ways to tell stories and control the narrative? First of all, take a moment to think of what stories are generally used for and how they play a part in people's everyday lives. While we may not always realize it, stories are essential to teaching us how to behave and what morals we should be following, and play just as big a role in the lives of adults as they do in the lives of children. The better told and more relatable a certain story is, the more firmly the lessons taught by that story will take hold in an individual's mind, and they will be more likely to adjust their behavior in response to the lessons learned from that story. The ultimate goal of telling a story should always be that the reader or listener will be motivated to change the way that they act after hearing the story. With this in mind, you can better learn how to tell stories that will benefit you and will help you exert influence over another person's mind. The most important aspect of whatever story you choose to tell should always be moral. The moral of the story is the lesson that the story is trying to teach its audience, and should always relate back to a certain behavior that you want your target to change or perform. Of course, there are a couple of reasons why you should hide the moral within a story rather than directly stating it to your target. The first reason is that morals are far more effective when they are used in a subtle way. Think of it like trying to make a dog take a pill: when you simply give the dog a plain pill, the dog wills most likely spit the pill back out. However, if you coat the pill in peanut butter, then the dog will happily eat the pill, many times without even realizing that there was ever a pill at all. When you simply tell someone that they are wrong about something and that you think that they should change their behavior, the other person is not going to take your opinion well, and will likely think that you are bossy and that you should mind your own business. When you hide your moral within a story, however, the message will not be absorbed as strongly within your target's consciousness, but rather it will stick in their subconsciousness, which will allow them to think about and internalize the moral of your story without realizing that you are telling them to do something, and they may not even realize that their behavior has changed as a result. Of course, simply using a story to express a moral is not enough to successfully implant your message within your target's mind without them realizing it. You have to be subtle when you are controlling the narrative, and you have to demonstrate your skill as a storyteller. If you make your stories too ridiculous or too hard for your target to follow, for example, then they will likely lose interest in your story and stop listening to it. In addition, if you make your moral too obvious, then the rest of the story no longer matters, and you will come off as preachy and smug, and your story will seem artificial. If you focus your time and skill on making your story simple, realistic, and above all else, subtle, then you will be much more effective at controlling the narrative.

Of course, when you are attempting to control the narrative, the stories you tell are not like stories as you might typically think of them. Stories used in controlling the narrative would not make good books or movies, for instance, and they generally work the best when they are short, sweet, and to the point. In their simplest form, stories are just slightly more complex lies. When you are controlling the narrative, you can make your story about yourself, or you can make your story about another person, who can either be real or completely made up. The only people you should generally avoid telling stories about are your target or people who your target has close relationships with, as stories about these people can easily be revealed to be false, and your target will likely end up being offended by them. When structuring your story, make sure that it follows two important rules: first that it relates back to whatever topic you and your target are talking about; and second, that your story makes logical sense. Stories are the most effective when they are used to add to and enhance a point that you are already in the process of making. When you bring up a story seemingly out of nowhere, the story is not compelling to your audience, and they have no reason to become invested in it. When you weave in a story with a related topic of conversation, however, the story adds to your authority and adds an element of social proof to your argument that is difficult to ignore.

The other thing to keep in mind when attempting to control the narrative is that the story that you are telling has to make logical sense. If your story does not make sense, then your target will not be able to relate to it, and will therefore not be affected by any moral that you choose to put in it. Of course, your story having to make sense is not the same thing as it having to be true, and as long as you keep all events in your story consistent, then you can have it be about anything that you want. Making your story short and precise will also help with making sure that it makes sense, as a shorter story will have fewer details that you have to keep track of. Creating a structure for your story to follow will also help you make sure that it makes logical sense. Good stories should have a beginning, middle, and an ending. The beginning is the part where you introduce your story to your target, the middle is where you lay out the events that occur during your story, and the ending should explain what happened as a result of those events. The ending should also be where you present the moral of your story. When your story follows a set beginning, middle, and ending, your target has a timeline of events to follow along with, which will help them relate more to the story. Having the moral be at the ending of the story also helps your target to remember the moral, as the ending will be the part of the story that they have most recently heard and the part that is the freshest in their mind.

Putting together all of these concepts can be tricky at first, but once you have learned how to construct a narrative and are comfortable with the process, you will find that you will be able to construct narratives on the fly without any prior planning at all. Of course, I know that this is a lot of information to keep in mind when you are first starting out, so I have created an example for you to refer to. For instance, if you are talking to a target and your goal is to get them to stop talking to somebody else, you can construct a narrative to accomplish your goal. You can say something along the lines of, "You know, I knew somebody that was good friends with that guy. They were close for a while, but it turns out he's kind of a jerk. Apparently, he gossips about other people all the time and says really horrible things about them behind their backs. My friend heard him talking about him, and it was bad enough that they don't talk anymore. I don't know everything about what happened, but I know that I would stay away from that guy." In order to understand what this story is getting at, let's break it down piece by piece. First is the beginning, which takes up the first two sentences. It introduces the person that you know and also sets up that the other guy is not a good person.

The middle takes up the next two sentences and brings up exactly what the other guy did that makes him a bad person. The last sentence is the ending and contains the moral: stay away from that other guy. The use of the phrases "apparently" and "I don't know everything about what happened" also give you an excuse to fall back on in case your target confronts the other person about what you have said. Through this example, you have planted seeds of doubt about this other person in your target's mind, warned them to stay away from the other person, and given yourself plausible deniability about the entire situation, all in just five sentences. In the context of a conversation, you can see where controlling the narrative is an invaluable strategy in controlling someone else's mind without them ever knowing.

When you are constructing a narrative, there are certain themes that you can use in your morals that are more powerful than other themes. Mind control is especially powerful when you are working towards a couple of different goals, most importantly isolation, criticism, and identity formation. While each of these concepts will be given an introduction here, they also share lots of overlap with hypnosis and brainwashing and will be discussed in greater detail in the following two chapters. Isolation is the act of keeping your target away from other people and any information that they might provide to your target. It can be carried out by physically keeping your target alone, but when used to achieve mind control, using nonphysical methods is far more effective and safer for you. The easiest way to bring about isolation through only the words that you use is by utilizing criticism. Criticism refers to when you associate any outside influences to your target with negative imagery, and can be even more effective when you both describe other people as negatively as possible while also referring to yourself in more positive terms. This will make your target prefer you and the information that you provide to them over anything from the outside and will draw them closer to you. Finally, the last concept that benefits from constructing a narrative are the formation of a new identity in your target. Forming a new identity is the most permanent concept that can occur using mind control, and will also make your target much easier for you to control. Controlling the narrative can help you shape your target's new identity to be what you want it to be, and once their new identity takes hold, they will become almost inseparable from you and what you want them to do.

Takeaways

While mind control, hypnosis, and brainwashing have similarities between them, mind control is the easiest for a beginner to manipulation to pull off consistently and successfully. By practicing controlling the narrative in addition to the other manipulation techniques that have already been discussed, you will be able to manipulate other people in a wide variety of situations and scenarios. For more powerful and longer-lasting techniques, however, you will have to learn more about hypnosis and brainwashing strategies. Be sure that you have a good understanding of all of the concepts and techniques that have been discussed up to this point before you move on, and as always, remember to keep up with practicing these techniques in order to improve. Mind control maybe the easiest concept to learn initially, but it is by no means easy to completely perfect, so do not be discouraged if you fail and be sure to keep on trying. As long as you remember to control the narrative in a smart, precise, and effective way, you will find at least some level of success.

Chapter 5: Hypnosis

If mind control is the best set of manipulation strategies for beginners to pick up and be able to learn quickly, then hypnosis is the next natural step in the process towards becoming a master of manipulation. In general, hypnosis lasts longer and is far more powerful than mind control is, although it also requires more skill to successfully pull off. While hypnosis has some concepts that overlap with mind control and brainwashing, it also has completely unique components, which can make it more challenging to learn. Hypnosis has a long a rich history, and today it is used in a wide variety of fields and industries, including in medicine, sports, psychotherapy, self-improvement, meditation and relaxation, forensics and criminal justice, art and literature, and the military. Of course, all instances of hypnosis share common characteristics no matter what context it is used in, and these same characteristics can come in handy when attempting to manipulate someone else. Having a good understanding of the principles and concepts of hypnosis can turn you from a mediocre manipulator into a highly skilled one.

The History of Hypnosis

Believe it or not, hypnotic techniques have been used for thousands of years, originating in India within the Hindu religion. The Hindus practiced a type of hypnosis called temple sleep, which they used to cure the sick and disabled who came to their temples. From there, hypnotic techniques were also discovered to have been used in Persia (modern-day Iran), Switzerland, Austria, Ireland, and Bavaria (now a part of Germany). However, hypnosis was not formally organized into science until the mid-1770s, when a scientist named Franz Anton Mesmer developed the theory of mesmerism, which stated that one person could exert control over another person through a magnetic force held within the body. While mesmerism was later proven to be largely untrue, parts of it were still found to be valid. Those parts were built upon by other scientists, the most notable of which was James Braid, a Scottish surgeon who first used the term "hypnosis" in his 1842 work, *Practical Essay on the Curative Agency of Neuro-Hypnotism*. Braid described hypnotism as "a peculiar condition of the nervous system, into which it may be thrown by artificial contrivance, and which differs, in several respects, from common sleep or the waking condition," which essentially means that rather than believing that hypnosis occurred as a result of a magnetic force, Braid believed that you could put someone in a hypnotic trance by manipulating their attention in specific ways. In 1843, he published the first book ever written on hypnosis, which he titled *Neurypnology*. After Braid's book was published, hypnotism began to be studied and used all over the world, especially in France, the United States, and decades later, Russia. As theories about hypnosis spread and began to grow, entire schools studying the subject began to pop up all over the world, the most famous of which was called the

Nancy School, which was located in France and directed by two different men, Ambroise-Auguste Liébeault and Hippolyte Bernheim. Liébeault and Bernheim were both physicians that had been trained in France, and contrary to popular opinion at the time, believed that anybody could be hypnotized under the right conditions. Many prominent scientists and psychologists in the 20th century, including Sigmund Freud, Clark L. Hull, and Milton Erickson, used the work done at the Nancy School to further develop their own theories. Erickson became extremely skilled in the use of hypnotic techniques, and later in his career founded the American Society of Clinical Hypnosis, which still operates today and offers courses and workshops for improving your own hypnotic expertise, as well as publishing the American Journal of Clinical Hypnosis. Through the end of the 20th century, hypnosis remained a popular topic to discuss, study, and research, and are still an important part of psychology and the study of behavioral responses today.

But why is knowing the history of hypnosis and its many forms helpful for actually learning the techniques associated with it? There are a couple of reasons. First of all, because the term "hypnosis" has gone through so many stages and forms meaning slightly different things, being more familiar with the history of hypnosis will help you know exactly what type of hypnosis you are dealing with. If, for example, you read about hypnosis being associated with magnetic, supernatural forces coming from within the body, you will know that you are reading about Franz Mesmer's work and that there are far more accurate theories of hypnosis that you could be reading about instead. Knowing even a little bit about the history of hypnosis can help you to avoid bad or even completely false information, which means that you can spend more time absorbing information that is actually useful and putting it into practice. Secondly, by knowing all about the way that hypnosis has evolved from definition to definition over the course of its lifetime, you will better understand that hypnosis is not necessarily a singular, fixed topic, and that there are many methods out there that you might find to be helpful if a certain concept is giving you too much trouble. The more theories of hypnosis that you learn about, the abler you are to find the one that works best for you. After spending a suitable amount of time practicing and studying hypnosis, you might even come up with your own theories!

Manipulation Technique #4: The Hypnotic Trance

At its core, hypnosis is all about planting ideas into somebody else's subconsciousness in order to influence their consciousness. If you manage to infiltrate a person's subconsciousness with enough skill, they will not be aware of what you are doing, and will never know that you ever influenced them at all. The best way to access someone's subconsciousness is to coax them into a relaxed, meditative state known as a hypnotic trance. Getting your target into a trance is the most difficult part of the process of hypnosis, but once you finally manage to pull it off, you will have a much easier time successfully manipulating them. Putting your target into a trance allows for you to have direct access to their subconsciousness, as their consciousness will no longer be an active part of their mind for the duration of the trance. The trace is what separates hypnosis from mind control, and the ability to induce it in somebody else is what separates a beginner of manipulation from a budding expert.

The best way to think of a hypnotic trance is a form of deep relaxation. You are likely already familiar with the overall concept of the trace, due to portrayals of hypnosis in book, movies, and popular culture in general. Of course, in real life, you cannot put somebody else into a hypnotic trance simply by waving a watch in front of their face or by using a magical code phrase that will put them to sleep. Instead, putting someone into a hypnotic trance takes lots of time and skill, and it may not always work on every single person that you try it out on, especially when you are first starting to attempt to use it. In fact, for the best introduction to the hypnotic trance, you may want to find a friend who is willing to allow you to put them into a trance in order to practice doing it, or if you cannot find someone who is a willing participant, you can always put yourself into a hypnotic trance using this same method. If you fail at putting somebody into a trance, you are likely to face a negative reaction from that person, as they are likely to recognize suspicious behavior when they see it if they still have full awareness of their surroundings. This is why it is important that you practice this technique several times before attempting it on any outsiders, as you are far more likely to succeed in putting somebody into a hypnotic trance if you have some familiarity with how it already works.

The first step in putting your target into a hypnotic trance is to make sure that they are in a sitting position, or even better, lying down. After all, once your target is in the trance and their consciousness has temporarily faded away, they will no longer physically be able to stand up or support the weight of their own body. An action as forceful and abrupt as falling on the floor will be enough to wake them up from the hypnotic trance, and once they have regained their awareness, they will likely want an explanation as to what happened. Obviously, this is not a situation that you want to be caught in, so it is important to make sure that your target's body is in a secure position that will not fall over or cause them to wake up once you have put them in the trance. This also means that you should not attempt to hypnotize anybody unless there is a couch, chairs, a bed, or another piece of comfortable furniture for your target to use. Convincing your target to sit or lay down sounds more difficult than it actually is. Remember that your target will be more likely to sit or lay down if a piece of furniture is offered to them to do so on and that you should be prepared to sit or lay down first, as your target will be more likely to do the same if they are following your lead. If all else fails, you can always mind control them and influence them to sit or lay down where you want them to. Do not worry too much about *how* you make your target get into the best position and instead focus your attention on what comes after you have already convinced them to do so.

The next step in the process of putting someone into a hypnotic trance is to get your target to listen to the sound of your voice. In hypnotic techniques, your voice can be a powerful tool as long as you know how to use it correctly. Take special note of the fact that this step does not instruct you to start a conversation with your target, but rather to get them to listen to you. This is because when attempting to put another person into a hypnotic trance, your voice is not being used to express any meaning or to describe any information, but rather as a way to create a sort of white noise, which will allow your target to slip further and further into a deeply relaxed state. If your target is engaged by what you are saying and tries to respond, then they are not letting go of their awareness, and their consciousness is still very much active. When attempting to put your target in a hypnotic trance, when you are first beginning to speak to them, the content of what you are saying matters a tremendous amount. You need to choose a topic that is interesting enough for them to want to stick around and listen to, but not so interesting that they are completely engrossed in what you are saying and are trying to speak back to you. The topic that you choose is likely to vary from target to target, as everyone has different tastes as to what kind of subject they are willing to pay attention to or not. This is where skills learned under controlling the narrative can come in handy; if you are able to tell a long, meandering story instead of a short and sweet one, especially about something that your target does not particularly care about, then they should begin falling into a hypnotic trance relatively easily. When you are speaking, be sure to use a calm, soothing voice, and choose words and phrases to use that are generally simple and easy to understand. This allows your target to focus on the overall sound of your voice, rather than what exactly you are saying. However, if you make your voice sound too calm and soothing, your target may think that something is wrong with you or may grow suspicious of your intentions. Therefore, try not to sound too much like a guided meditation instructor and instead attempt to model your voice in the style of the narrator of a nature documentary. Keep in mind that your goal is to relax your target, but not to put them to sleep. If you make yourself sound too soothing, you will run the risk of having your target be too relaxed. If your target is asleep, after all, they will not be open to any suggestions that you make, as they will be unconscious. Once you see that your target has fallen into a more and more relaxed state, the content of what you are saying to them will not matter as much, and as long as you keep your voice in a steady, soothing tone, you will not have to worry about what topic you are speaking about any longer.

In addition to using your voice as white noise, there are some other techniques that you can use in order to lull your target into a hypnotic trance. One trick is to have your target eat or drink something before you attempt to put them in a trance. Whatever they consume will be more effective if it is easy to digest and is warmer rather than colder. Eating or drinking something will cause your target's body to allocate resources and energy to digest what they have consumed, which will take resources away from their overall energy levels and will cause them to feel more tired and sleepy as a result. Be sure that they do not eat or drink too much of a substance, since feeling too full will cause them to focus on that feeling rather than on you. Another trick that you can use to better put someone into a hypnotic trance is to turn on relaxing music. Music is another excellent source of white noise, so long as the music is itself relaxing and easy to listen to. In general, the more simple the music is, the better the white noise that it makes. For example, you should consider using solo piano tracks with a relatively simple melody over tracks that feature many different instruments and voices with loud, energetic melodies. Music that you may use should follow the same principles as your voice: it should be soothing and easy to listen to, but not so simple that your target will grow bored of it. You should also keep in mind that not everyone is relaxed by too much noise and some people may even be distracted by any music that you decide to play, so music is not always an effective tool in hypnosis. Finally, another easy trick to use is making sure that the temperature is comfortable for your target. While you do not always have control over what the temperature feels like, if you can ensure that the temperature is always at a normal level and would be comfortable to fall asleep in, you will have a much easier time with putting your target in a hypnotic trance. If the temperature is too hot or too cold, your target will be unable to sufficiently relax, and their awareness will always be affected too much by their surroundings for it to ever fade away.

You can tell if you have successfully put your target in a trance or not based on what they look like. If they appear to be in a deep sleep, taking deep breaths and are completely unaware of what is going on around them, then they are most likely in a trance. Once you believe that your target is in a hypnotic trance, you can begin to ask them questions and influence their subconsciousness. The first questions you ask should be to determine whether or not your target is in a trance. For instance, good questions would include things such as, "Do you know where you are?" and "Do you feel relaxed?" Asking yes-or-no questions is a good way to let your target ease into their trance while still providing you with answers. If your target says that they feel relaxed and that they do not know where they are, then they are in a hypnotic trance, and you can begin to influence them in whatever direction that you like. Remember that while your target is in a trance, suggestions are powerful, and while you should never state outright what it is you want your target to do, you can strongly hint at your goal, which they will pick up on in their subconsciousness. There are two methods of changing the speech patterns that you can use in order for your suggestions to be more effective while your target is in a trance. First of all, you should phrase your statements in the form of a question, which allows your target's subconsciousness to form an answer, therefore planting the statement and the answer in your target's mind. This works best if you can phrase your question in such a way that would be ridiculous or even impossible to say no to. As long as you know your target's personality and individual preferences, tailoring questions to their own judgment should not be difficult to accomplish. Secondly, when speaking, you should try to integrate storytelling techniques along with your suggestions. Using vivid imagery in your speech will help your target's subconsciousness better visualize what you are talking about, and it will be more likely to latch onto your suggestions as a result. The easier you make your suggestions for your target to understand, the more successful you will be in influencing them.

When you are ready to wake your target from their trance, simply talk them back to a state of awareness. For example, you could say something along the lines of, "I know you are feeling very sleepy now, but as I talk to you, you will begin to feel more and more awake. I am going to count to three, and by the time I am finished, your eyes will be open, and you will be awake. One...two...three." When your target is awake, they will likely be confused about what has happened. They will not remember anything that you told them while they were in the trance, and they will not be aware that they were in a trance at all. You can tell them that they simply fell asleep, and you can even joke with them about the occasion. In the days after the trance, they will begin to perform behaviors that are in line with what you instructed them to do during the trance. During this time, keep in contact with them, and influence them further with mind control and NLP techniques as needed. If they are not making as much progress as you would like them to, you can always put them in another trance and make more suggestions. Try to avoid putting somebody in a trance too many times, however, as they will eventually catch on to the fact that they have not been simply falling asleep. Of course, a singular trance is generally enough to manipulate a target and see successful results come out of it.

Manipulation Technique #5: Choose Your Targets Wisely

As I mentioned earlier, not everyone is as vulnerable to being hypnotized as other people, and a small percentage of people are not able to be hypnotized successfully at all. On the other hand, some people can become hypnotized quite easily, and the effects of hypnosis are far more powerful on them. With so much variety within the human population, how are you supposed to choose targets? There are many different factors to keep an eye out for, and over the course of time, you will find people with certain characteristics that personally work better with the habits and techniques that you find to be most useful. Of course, when you are just starting out at manipulation and hypnosis, choosing a target to influence can be incredibly overwhelming. Fortunately, there are three common factors that you should look out for no matter what level your hypnosis skills are at: the target's (1) personal life, (2) personality, and (3) relationship to you.

In general, a target's personal life cannot be influenced by you and should be considered baggage that comes with a potential target. If the target has a stable personal life with several strong relationships with other people, they are not going to be a strong candidate for hypnosis. The more support a person has in their life, the more influences they are going to encounter outside of you, meaning that your input is competing with many other inputs and does not matter that much. If, on the other hand, a target is largely isolated from other people and frequently comes into contact with stress and conflict, they will be much more vulnerable to hypnosis. Instability in another person's life gives you the opportunity to be a shoulder for them to lean on, and they will form a much stronger, more trusting bond with you than if they had other outlets in life.

Just like with their personal life, a target's personality cannot be changed by you, unless you dedicate enormous amounts of time to doing so, and even then only small changes will be achieved. There are certain personality traits that determine whether or not a person is a good target for being hypnotized. Some people, for instance, are more open and trusting than other people, which makes them better targets for manipulation. People who are superstitious and believe in a supernatural activity such as ghosts and aliens are also more able to be hypnotized than people who are more skeptics. In general, you should avoid trying to hypnotize anyone who is extremely intelligent or possesses any of the traits in the Dark Triad, as these people are not only less able to be manipulated, but the consequences for attempting to manipulate them can be dire.

A potential target's relationship with you is unique in that it is entirely influenced by you. The stronger your relationship to a potential target is, the more effective any hypnosis or manipulation techniques will be on them. Think of a relationship as an exchange of information. The more information you have about a target, the better you will understand how their mind works, which is an invaluable part of the hypnosis process. In addition, people that you have a strong relationship with are less likely to be suspicious of you, meaning that you can try riskier, more advanced manipulation techniques on these people without them necessarily believing that you are doing anything at all. If you cultivate a relationship for long periods of time, you can also manipulate your target for that much longer, as you will have routine contact with them and can reinforce any and all of your influences on them on a regular basis.

Takeaways

Hypnosis can certainly be both difficult to learn and difficult to master, but at the same time, it is generally the most powerful option of manipulation available to you with the lowest amount of risk. While brainwashing is more effective and it lasts longer, it can be incredibly risky to attempt, which makes hypnosis an extremely valuable technique for experienced manipulators. As with all other techniques discussed in this book, the key to truly mastering hypnotism is to practice well and practice often. The more experience you gain with hypnosis, the more effectively you will be able to use it. As long as you know the history and the techniques of hypnosis, you should be able to find success when putting it all into practice. Be sure that you have a solid understanding of the ins and outs of hypnotism before continuing on to the next chapter, which will discuss brainwashing and its techniques in detail.

Chapter 6: Brainwashing

Brainwashing as a manipulation technique is far more powerful than both mind control and hypnosis, but it also requires far more training and expertise in order to be used in the most effective way. While many of the concepts used in hypnosis and mind control overlap with those of brainwashing, there are also new techniques made available to you when you learn about brainwashing. Just like hypnosis, brainwashing is a popular topic and plot device in many books, movies, and other media. Of course, as well as being the most powerful technique, brainwashing is also more high-profile than both hypnosis and mind control, and has been used extensively in certain large-scale scenarios, including by certain governments, cults, corporations, and in other instances. While brainwashing has been known throughout history by many different names, including thought reform, thought control, coercive persuasion, re-education, and menticide, for the sake of simplicity, this chapter will only refer to it as brainwashing. By learning more about what brainwashing is and how it actually works, you will not only have gained a valuable technique for manipulating other people, but you will also be able to more easily recognize when you are being brainwashed by another person or by an organization.

The History of Brainwashing

One of the most well-known portrayals of brainwashing on a massive scale in fiction is found in the book *1984*, which was written by George Orwell in 1949. In the book, a massive government entity maintains complete control over its citizens by creating propaganda, using surveillance to spy on people, rationing food, and even training people to use a different language. There is no magical technology that allows the government to directly control the thoughts and actions of its citizens, but through the laws it creates and the way that it enforces those laws, it can make its citizens think and act in only the ways that it wants them to. Even though *1984* is a work of fiction, governments like the one described in the book have certainly existed in real life, and still, continue to do so today. Of course, brainwashing has been used by other organizations than governments in its history, and different groups have used brainwashing successfully in different ways in order to further their goals.

While certain forms of brainwashing techniques have been in use for thousands of years, the public did not become aware of brainwashing on a large scale until the 1940s and the 1950s. At that time, brainwashing was a major part of society in China under Mao Zedong, the Chairman of the Communist Party of China and the leader of China overall. In fact, the term "brainwashing" comes from the Chinese phrase *xǐnǎo*, which literally translates to "wash brain" in English. Americans were not made aware of brainwashing as a phenomenon until after the Korean War had begun.

During the war, American soldiers were captured as prisoners of war (POWs), and during their time spent in Chinese prison facilities, they were brainwashed by the Chinese government. The POWs that had been brainwashed were more likely to give over classified information to the Chinese and give false confessions, more willing to do what their captors wanted them to, and even defended the actions of the Chinese government. The United Nations commander at the time stated that "too familiar are the mind-annihilating methods of these Communists in extorting whatever words they want…The men themselves are not to blame, and they have my deepest sympathy for having been used in this abominable way." In other words, the Chinese were extremely skilled at brainwashing their victims, who would feel the effects of being brainwashed for years after it had been done to them. After American POWs were found to have been brainwashed, the United States Central Intelligence Agency (CIA) ran a series of experiments over the span of twenty years that tested mind control and brainwashing capabilities, the most famous of these experiments being called Project MKUltra. In addition, to testing general brainwashing techniques, the CIA also experimented with drugs as a tool for manipulation and attempted to create a so-called truth serum that would be used for interrogation purposes. Both the Chinese brainwashing institutions and the CIA experiments will be discussed in greater detail in the following chapter, but as they are an essential part of the history of brainwashing, it is important that they are mentioned here as well.

From there, brainwashing took hold in the minds of the public and began to play a large part in popular culture. Stories involving brainwashing were received by large audiences, and movies such as *The Fearmakers*, *Toward the Unknown*, *The Bamboo Prison*, *The Rack*, and most famously, *The Manchurian Candidate* were all inspired in some part by the experience of American POWs during the war or brainwashing in general. Beginning in the late 1960s and extending through the mid-1970s, brainwashing as a concept was so deeply rooted in the public consciousness that it even seeped into the criminal justice system. Perhaps the most famous example is that of Patty Hearst, an heiress who was kidnapped and brainwashed by a terrorist group known as the Symbionese Liberation Army (SLA). She later joined the group as a member and was arrested during an attempted bank robbery. Her trial was the first widely publicized instance of using brainwashing as a legal defense in court, and while she was ultimately found guilty, the defense caused a renewal of interest in and concern over brainwashing.

Since the 1960s, brainwashing has also been widely used in recruiting members to cults. The most well-known instance of brainwashing being used in cults is probably that of the Manson Family, founded in 1967 by Charles Manson. Manson was an extremely skilled manipulator, and successfully recruited nearly 100 people, mostly women, into his own cult following. He had such a strong influence over them that he was able to convince them to commit a number of different crimes, from assault and robbery all the way to mass murder. Nearly all cults use some form of brainwashing to indoctrinate potential recruits and convince them to join, from the most infamous to cults you have never heard of before. Some cults, such as Heaven's Gate and The People's Temple, used brainwashing to such a powerful effect that their followers were convinced to commit suicide. Cults are especially important to study in regard to brainwashing because they demonstrate how far the power of brainwashing techniques can really take people and are a good indicator of when things have gone too far. Obviously, if you are thinking of using brainwashing or any other type of manipulation on a person in order to make them inflict harm on themselves or anyone else, you should refrain from doing so and seek professional help for yourself.

But why is the history of brainwashing so important to learn about? After all, you are not a government entity such as the Communist Party of China, and you are hopefully not planning on dabbling in becoming a cult leader of any kind. Of course, there are valuable lessons to be learned from the history of brainwashing that you can apply to how you approach and implement brainwashing techniques in your own life. First of all, having a good understanding of the history of brainwashing should mean that you also have a good understanding of just how powerful brainwashing can be, even on the most unwilling targets. If American soldiers can be brainwashed into defending their captors, enemies of the country that they vowed to serve, then imagine what brainwashing can do for you if used correctly. Secondly, the history of brainwashing teaches the important lesson that unlike mind control and hypnosis, anybody and everybody are susceptible to brainwashing techniques. If you focus on honing your talents and become a skilled enough manipulator, you can brainwash not just one person, but multiple people at a time into doing whatever it is that you want for them to do. The most talented manipulators can exert their influence over hundreds of people all at once, and each and every single one of their targets will be as thoroughly indoctrinated as the last one. This leads me into the final reason why the history of brainwashing is important to have at least some knowledge of because brainwashing is such a powerful and effective tool that can be used on so many people, it can be easy to take brainwashing too far, and force your targets into criminal or even life-threatening situations. By studying the history of brainwashing, you will know how horrible the effects of brainwashing can be for the target, the manipulator, and for anybody else who gets caught in between. While brainwashing as a tactic is not in and of itself harmful, when used with reckless abandon, things can quickly spiral out of control. As the manipulator, it is your responsibility to know when to stop before something terrible has occurred. Above all else, the history of brainwashing demonstrates the need to be safe, sensible, and responsible when using brainwashing techniques, as the consequences can be dire if brainwashing is used irresponsibly.

Manipulation Technique #6: Isolation, Criticism, and Identity Formation

Isolation, criticism, and identity formation are essential concepts for any aspiring manipulator to be very familiar with. These three topics are extremely important not only in brainwashing but in the art of manipulation overall. While these three topics were already mentioned briefly in Chapter 5, they will be expanded upon here, so that you have a full and complete understanding of them before attempting any brainwashing techniques or strategies.

Isolation refers to the act of separating your target from any external information or stimuli that they might receive, particularly when that information comes from people other than yourself. The ultimate objective of isolation is to make yourself the main provider of information in your target's life, as that way you can expressly choose which particular types of information that they might have access to in order to better control them. Of course, you cannot ever control each and every single piece of information that your target has access to, but isolation will help you to not only control as much of that information as possible but also to control the narrative about any information that you do not control in order to downplay its importance to and impact on your target.

There are two different ways that isolation can be accomplished. The first method of isolation is physical. This method is fairly straightforward: placing physical barriers between your target and information that you do not want them to have access to is relatively simple and theoretically easy to accomplish. An example of physical isolation would be locking your target in a room, which would contain only information that you would want to share with them. Of course, with this example, you can also easily see the downside of physical isolation, which is that it is often illegal and will almost certainly backfire on you at some point. Therefore, physical isolation should be used sparingly, and only in situations that do not violate any laws or the rights of your target. The other method of isolation, nonphysical isolation, is more subtle and difficult to successfully pull off but will be the more useful option available to you a majority of the time.

Nonphysical isolation is accomplished through mind control methods such as manipulating beliefs, controlling the narrative, and through the use of criticism, as well as through the principles of persuasion and deception. At its core, nonphysical isolation is not about actually placing restrictions upon a person and the information that they have access to, but rather making them believe that there are restrictions in place. Planting that belief in your target is crucial, since if they believe that a certain type of information is not legitimate or that certain people are not good friends to them, then they will begin to monitor their own behavior, rather than you having to do it for them. This is especially useful at times when you cannot be around your target for whatever reason, as you can still be certain that they are not receiving information from sources that may undermine your goals.

One of the most useful tools to achieve isolation is called criticism. Used in the context of dark psychology, criticism refers to something slightly different than what you might be used to. Criticism is best used when you criticize the world around you and your target, rather than criticizing the target themselves. When you point out everything that is harmful and untrustworthy in the world around you, by default you will make yourself seem more trustworthy to your target. After all, if you are both smart enough to be able to see everything wrong with the outside world and also do not point out anything that is wrong with yourself, then your target will assume that there is nothing that is wrong with you and decide to trust you. Of course, you do not have to be entirely honest when you are using criticism, and you may find it effective to criticize certain things that might actually not have anything wrong with them. The principles of persuasion and deception can be very useful when using criticism, as they will make your claims be even more convincing to your target. As long as you can make the world around you seem unsafe and untrustworthy while making yourself seem to be a positive influence, your target will naturally gravitate towards you rather than gathering information from the outside world, and you will have achieved nonphysical isolation on your target.

When you are performing any kind of manipulation strategy, whether that would be NLP techniques, mind control, hypnosis, brainwashing, or some combination of several strategies, your ultimate goal should always be to form a new identity within your target. Identity formation is the most permanent type of manipulation that you can pull off, as it ensures that your target will be deeply connected with you for the foreseeable future, as long as you do not make any mistakes or allow any other new identities to take hold within them. Identity formation is the most effective when you use frequent repetition on your target. When you are attempting to form a new identity within your target, you should follow three steps: (1) isolate your target, (2) seek verbal confirmation from your target, and (3) test your target's new identity.

The first step, isolates your target, should be fairly straightforward to you now and involves everything that was discussed in the previous two paragraphs. Isolating your target is critical to forming a new identity within your target, as it allows for you and you alone to shape whatever you want their new identity to become. Remember that isolation takes time, and if you rush the process, you may risk your target catching on to what you are attempting to do and losing any connection you might have already established with them.

The second step is to seek verbal confirmation from your target. It can be difficult to tell when a target has been sufficiently isolated, and the best way to tell if a new identity has begun to take hold within them is to simply ask them. Of course, you should not ask them about any changes in their identity directly. Rather, you should ask them how they feel about you, and specifically whether they think you are a good person or not. Controlling the narrative can come in handy here, as you can craft a story where you might have been having doubts about your own self-worth or morality, and your target will rush in to reassure you about your own worth. Having your target state that they believe that you are a good person might seem like a small thing, but it is actually a major milestone for two reasons. First of all, having your target say the words themselves is far more powerful than them listening to you say them and proves that the belief is rooted deep within their subconsciousness.

Secondly, by admitting that you are a good person, they will be more likely to go along with whatever you want in the future, as they will not want to have their statement proven to be wrong. Accepting this first statement will lead to them accepting more and more in the future. This leads to the final step, which is to test your target's new identity. This step sounds complicated, but it can actually be quite simple. All you have to do is ask your target to carry out some action related to their new identity. While the second step is all about a verbal commitment, the final step requires a change in behavior, which is much more serious. It is one thing to talk about new beliefs; it is another thing entirely to act upon those new beliefs. By choosing a relatively small and unimportant task for your target to carry out, you can make it easier on them to change their behavior. Just like with the second step, your target will be more likely to move on to bigger and more involved actions after they have first committed to something small, as they will not want to be proven wrong about you. Once they have performed some kind of task for you, you can be assured that even if their new identity has not been entirely formed yet, then it is well on its way, and your work as a manipulator will be almost finished.

Manipulation Technique #7: Managing Your Target's Expectations

Contrary to many popular depictions of the brainwashing process, brainwashing is, at its core, actually very simple. Above all else, brainwashing is about managing your target's expectations. Exactly how you manage your target's expectations is up to you, but there are certain factors that you should keep in mind when attempting to brainwash a target. The process of brainwashing can be divided up into three steps, with managing your target's expectations being essential in each one. The first step is known as the introduction and refers to how you present yourself to your target upon first meeting them. If your target is somebody that you already have a prior relationship with, do not worry; while the introduction will not necessarily apply to you, you can still manage your target's expectations and follow the other two steps. The introduction serves as the chance for you to make a first impression on your target, and present yourself as somebody that your target will want to get to know more closely. If your introduction is the first time that you have met your target, then managing your target's expectations will be easy, as they will likely not know what to expect from you, meaning that you will be free to present as whoever and whatever you choose to be. However, if you have a prior relationship with your target, then you will have to take a far more active role in managing their expectations. If your relationship is positive and they already trust you, of course, then you will not have to put in the work of an introduction. However, if your prior relationship is negative, not very close, or a combination of the two, then you will have to work to change that relationship for the better.

For example, if you have offended your target in the past in any way, be sure to apologize, and show them that you are no longer that same person. Similarly, if your target is only familiar with you through unflattering rumors or gossip about you, then it is up to you to prove to them that those rumors are false. Whatever you have to do in order to fix your relationship with your target, do so. Remember that other mind control techniques can help you in this respect.

The second step in the brainwashing process is to build trust between your target and you. This step is where your role in managing your target's expectations should expand. In addition to managing your target's expectations about yourself, you must also begin to manage their expectations about the world around them. This step is the most time-consuming in the brainwashing process, but it is also the most crucial. A bad introduction can always be repaired, but if there is no trust between your target and you, then you will not be able to manipulate them. The easiest way to build trust is through the use of isolation. If you can convince your target not only that you are a good influence on them, but that the rest of the world is potentially dangerous and harmful to them, then your power over your target will be greatly increased. Not only will you have built trust between your target and yourself, but you will have also created a situation in which they depend on you as their main source of information, which will pave the way for you to manipulate them however you want in the future. Another good way of building trust is through controlling the flow of information that your target receives in a very precise, particular way. You should always start off by feeding your target small and uncontroversial pieces of information that are easy to understand, then work your way up to bigger pieces of information that might be harder for your target to accept. By starting small, you are conditioning your target to accept whatever it is you say, which will make it easier for them to follow your lead when you move on to ideas or beliefs that your target would previously have been more likely to have an issue with. Whatever method you choose to use, remember that the more time you spend building trust between your target and you, the easier it will be to successfully manipulate them, and the more likely they will end up forming a new identity that revolves around you and your influence.

The final step in the brainwashing process is to test your target. Testing your target allows for you to see if you have managed your target's expectations to a sufficient degree or if there are still things left that you need to tweak. This step works in a similar way to testing a target's new identity formation, and if you are skilled enough, you can use the same test to check on both a target's identity and if they are brainwashed or not. The test that you choose should not ask too much of your target, but should also be something that they would not normally do if they were not brainwashed. For example, if you know that your target does not like the taste of a certain food, ask them to eat that food in front of you. If they follow your instructions, then the process is complete, while if they refuse, then you will have to further manage your target's expectations. If your target fails the test, do not become angry with them; instead, focus on what things you need to change before they will listen to you. On the other hand, if your target passes the test, remember that your work is not over; brainwashing is strong, but it does not last forever, and you will have to continue to monitor your target and manage their expectations according to what you want to occur.

Takeaways

Now that you have read all about mind control, hypnosis, and brainwashing, you are well on your way to becoming a master manipulator. Do not feel the need to treat these methods as absolute laws, and if you find something different that works better for you, do not be afraid to use that instead. Most importantly, keep in mind that with great power comes great responsibility, and never put your target in a situation where they pose a danger to themselves or to others. Read on to find out more about how manipulation techniques have been used for both the good and the bad.

Chapter 7: Case Studies

After reading this far, you are now familiar with the techniques associated with the principles of NLP, mind control, hypnosis, and brainwashing, and you might have even begun to put these techniques into action. Of course, having a few examples to see how these techniques are used in the real world can be hugely beneficial in understanding how to use and improve your skills of manipulation even more. This chapter will be taking an in-depth look at three ways that manipulation techniques have either been used in the past or are being used today: the use of NLP techniques in modern medicine, how thought reform was used by the communist Chinese government, and the experiments the CIA carried out in order to study brainwashing. These case studies are meant to help bolster your understanding of manipulation techniques as a whole, and while they might not line up exactly with what you are attempting to do with these techniques, they should allow to you see the possibilities offered by these techniques in an entirely new way.

These examples can also help to illustrate the dangers of manipulation techniques when they are taken too far. While it is not necessary to know every detail of the case studies discussed in this chapter, if you want to improve your abilities and become a master manipulator, you should at least be familiar with these examples.

Case Study #1: NLP Techniques in Modern Medicine

You might remember that way back in a section from Chapter 1, the history of how NLP was developed and first used was discussed. You might also remember from that section that one of the ways NLP techniques were first advertised was as a way to cure various mental illnesses, including anxiety, depression, certain learning disorders, and overwhelming, unreasonable phobias. While NLP techniques later became more well-known in fields such as business and education, a dedicated group of therapists, psychologists, and other medical professionals continued to develop and perfect NLP techniques for use in medicine and therapy. Today, NLP techniques are used in a specialized setting in order to treat mental illnesses and have grown increasingly popular with people seeking treatment all over the world. But how do NLP techniques actually work in treating mental illnesses, and how is it relevant at all to develop your skills of manipulation? After all, it probably seems like NLP techniques used in a medicinal setting are completely different from techniques used in order to influence somebody else. However, these two fields have more in common than you might expect, and understanding the uses of NLP techniques in medicine might give you some new ideas to use when you are attempting to manipulate someone else.

When NLP techniques are used in a medicinal setting, they take place between a medical professional (usually a therapist, psychologist, or psychiatrist) and their patient. In this setting, the professional's use of NLP techniques on the patient is always consensual, as the patient is expressly seeking treatment in the form of NLP, so manipulation methods such as isolation are not necessary for the professional to use. Instead, they use NLP in medicine relies more on techniques that are similar to manipulating beliefs and controlling the narrative, but are just different enough to make them unique. The key difference is the patient's willingness to submit to NLP techniques, which allows for the medical professional and their patent to work together to come up with personalized strategies for the professional to use on the patient. This gives the medical professional an edge over someone in the role of the manipulator, as the manipulator cannot speak openly to their target about what strategies might work best for them. This advantage also allows for the NLP strategies used by the medical professional to be used on the patient much more quickly than a manipulator could use the same strategies on a target, as the manipulator has to spend far more time gathering information about the target in the form of learning than the medical professional does.

The NLP techniques that are used by a medical professional are also different from those used by a manipulator in their content. As you are already familiar with, techniques used by a manipulator depend heavily on information, in particular controlling what information a target does and does not have access to in order to accomplish a goal such as manipulating a target's beliefs. As a manipulator, if you cannot adequately and skillfully use the information to your advantage, then successfully manipulating a chosen target will almost certainly be impossible to do. On the other hand, when NLP techniques are used by a medical professional, then the concept of visualization is more important than the use of information. The term "visualization" refers to the images that a target (or in a medical setting, patient) sees in their mind when they are processing information. In other words, the precise use of information is most important in the use of NLP for manipulation, while the way in which information is processed is most important in a medical context. In a medicinal setting, visualization is extremely important for two reasons. First of all, because the medical professional and the patent are working together in order to change something about the patient's mental illness, the patient already has access to most, if not all, of the information being used in the procedure, so controlling that information in a precise way is not possible. Therefore, the medical professional has to work harder to change the patient's prior thoughts and feelings about that information, which is where visualization comes in. Secondly, visualization allows for the patient to make better comparisons of information that they already have. When treating mental illness with NLP techniques, a medical professional will generally want a patient to compare a bad part of their life, such as how their mental illness makes them feel, with a good part of their life, such as any achievements or accomplishments the patient might have earned. Visualization allows the patient to better understand what separates the good from the bad, as well as what they can work on changing in order to turn the bad parts into something more positive.

You might already be beginning to see how you can use the principles of NLP techniques used in a medicinal setting to improve your own manipulation skills. There are a couple of different lessons to be learned from the use of NLP by medical professionals. The first lesson is that you should always work to have the strongest relationship with your target possible before you attempt any serious manipulation strategies on them. One of the main reasons why NLP techniques are so effective in treating mental illnesses is because the medical profession and the patient have a high level of trust between them, and while you cannot necessarily be as honest with your target as a medical professional can be with their patient, you should still certainly focus on building a good relationship between yourself and your target. The second lesson is that while information is extremely important to the process of manipulation, the way the target processes that information can be just as valuable to you. Even if you do not necessarily use visualization as part of your manipulation techniques, the fact that NLP techniques used for medicinal purposes are so effective should impress upon you the importance of doing more than simply controlling the flow of information. Finally, the third lesson you should take away from this example is how critical it is to have an end goal in mind when you are using manipulation techniques on another person. I know that this seems like it should be obvious, but you would be surprised at how often people are so focused on the process of manipulation that they forget about what they actually want to accomplish. When NLP techniques are used for medicinal purposes, the end goal is always to treat the patent's mental illness, and every single action that the medical professional takes is done in order to fulfill that end goal. You should keep a similar philosophy in mind when using NLP techniques and other methods of manipulation on your target: do not rush the process, but remember that every step you take should lead you closer to a final goal.

Case Study #2: Thought Reform in Communist China

As mentioned in Chapter 6, thought reform, which is also known as brainwashing, was used in China under the rule of Mao Zedong and the Communist Party in order to make both citizens and American POWs accept the government's control and its ideology. The thought reform campaign was so successful that when POWs had been returned safely home, they still defended their Chinese captors and thought that they had been doing the right thing all along. The government started the thought reform campaign by targeting Chinese scholars, professors, and teachers, urging them to accept Marxism-Leninism over more traditionally European-American schools of thought. From there, the teachers taught Marxism-Leninism to students, and the government's chosen ideology spread throughout the educated populace and eventually through Chinese businesses, peasant organizations, and even prisons until nearly the entire population was brainwashed into accepting the government's ideology. The government's goal was to create a population made up of what was called the "New Socialist Man," which referred to embracing a communist revolution and an entirely new way of life, as well as being loyal to the Communist Party, participating in labor activities, showing no signs of selfishness, and having a heightened awareness of the class system in China. American POWs were brainwashed to accept and conform to the model of the New Socialist Man, as well as being brainwashed into giving the Chinese critical intelligence about the Korean War. A psychiatrist named Dr. Robert J. Lifton worked closely with brainwashed POWs that returned from the war and learned about how the Chinese used thought reform so successfully in the process. He identified eight distinct criteria for thought reform.

The first criteria for thought reform are known as "milieu control." Milieu control refers to controlling a person's environment in order to achieve isolation. Controlling a target's environment ultimately limits what information that they receive, which leads them to become overly dependent on whoever is controlling the environment (in this case, the Chinese government). It also pushes the target away from society as a whole, resulting in a population that is highly isolated from one another and therefore easily controllable.

Lifton called the second criteria for thought reform "mystical manipulation." Despite how it sounds, mystical manipulation does not refer to any real supernatural event. Instead, it simply refers to the act of faking such events in order to prove that you have some kind of special talent or ability, which results in you obtaining a status of authority. You can then use that authority to create more planned "supernatural" events or to take a more active role in religious life. Mystical manipulation was most often used to claim that a person or group had been chosen by God to lead everybody else, which gave that person or group the authority to do nearly anything that they wanted.

The third criteria for thought reform are known as a "demand for purity." Demand for purity refers to the need for targets to view the world in uncomplicated, black and white terms. There is no room for doubt or vagueness in the target's mind; everything must either be right or wrong. Demand for purity is most useful when it is used to control a group rather than an individual, as the group will enforce the rules and punish anyone who does not conform to the terms outlined in the demand for purity.

The fourth criteria identified by Lifton are known as "confession." Just like a demand for purity, confession is also most useful when used within the context of a group of people rather than an individual. Confession is best understood in terms of "sins," meaning a person's innermost thoughts, feelings, and attitudes. Sins are confessed openly to the group, and no secrets can be safe for long. The group's leaders use this information to their advantage and use the dynamics of the group to exploit members who might cause trouble.

The fifth criteria for thought reform are known as "sacred science." Once again, sacred science works best when it is used to control the behavior of a group of people rather than an individual. Sacred science refers to the principle that within a group there is a dominant ideology, and that any other competing ideology is completely wrong and invalid. Outside groups are also completely invalid simply because they do not belong within the "correct" group. In a similar vein, the leader of the group cannot be criticized or disagreed with, and their word is taken as law.

The sixth criteria for thought reform are known as "loading the language," which involves using new words and phrases in a specific way in order to confuse outsiders. This way, certain groups can remain separate from other groups while also manipulating the terms in which their members think about and process information, which grants the leaders of the group a large degree of control over everybody else. Loading the language also makes it very difficult for current members of a certain group to leave and join a different group, particularly if they have been a member of the group for a long period of time and/or through formative years, as they will have a hard time understanding the way the outside world communicates and struggle to adapt accordingly.

Lifton's seventh criteria for thought reform are known as "doctrine over person." Doctrine over a person is relatively easy to understand, as it mostly supplements the other criteria rather than being its own distinct idea. Doctrine over person refers to the idea that an individual's own, personal experiences mean nothing unless they fit within the ideology of the group. In other words, experiences must fit into the sacred science in order to be considered valid, and if they do not fit, then the experiences are considered not to have happened at all.

The eighth and final criteria for thought reform are known as "dispensing of existence." Dispensing of existence is the most powerful criteria out of all of them and should not be taken lightly. Dispensing of existence simply means that a group (or more specifically, a group's leaders) is in charge of determining what is allowed to exist and what is not. This does not mean that the group terminates or kills anything that it decides does not exist; rather, dispensing of existence takes on a more advanced form of shunning, in which the group ignores the presence of anything that it has determined does not exist. Anybody who leaves the group is also removed from existence in the minds of the remaining group members. Dispensing of existence applies to oppose ideas, groups, and even individuals, which makes it difficult to rescue anybody from a group that has been influenced by thought reform, as members will ignore anything that opposes their sacred science.

So what lessons can be learned from the use of thought reform in communist China? First of all, this example shows the extreme power that brainwashing can have if used in a skillful and methodical manner. The Communist Party of China managed to not only brainwash their entire population through the use of thought reform, but they were also able to influence people who came from entirely different culture using the same process as well. Although a singular manipulator lacks the power of a government, you can certainly see how thought reform could be used to influence multiple people at once. This leads into the second lesson learned from this case study: brainwashing is more effective when it is used on a group of people all at the same time rather on individuals. While you can absolutely brainwash singular targets, certain tactics are far more effective within a group, as you can shape the group dynamics to become self-enforcing. This can pressure members of the group to follow the group's ideology, which you can determine as the leader of the group. The third lesson is, of course, the eight new techniques described as Lifton's criteria for thought reform. While you may not be able to use all of these during the brainwashing process, and indeed not all of them are always necessary to use, you will likely find the eight criteria for thought reform very useful to keep in mind when using manipulation techniques, especially when you are working within a group setting.

Case Study #3: The CIA Brainwashing Experiments

After American POWs came home from the Korean War, people were shocked to witness how effectively the Chinese government had altered their personalities and their loyalties, and many wanted answers as to how such a thing could have happened. American government officials sought answers just like everybody else, but they also wanted to learn how to harness and improve brainwashing techniques for themselves so that the United States could gain an edge in the developing Cold War. Both the CIA and the Department of Defense created a series of experiments in order to determine the manipulation techniques used by the Chinese and went on to involve different settings and elements, most notoriously the use of mind-altering drugs. The CIA went on to develop Project MKUltra, which was created in order to produce a "truth serum" that could be used on people who were suspected of being Soviet or Chinese spies. Brainwashing experiments took place on both American and Canadian citizens, and the CIA's ultimate goal was to gain control over foreign leaders and manipulate them into instituting policies that were far friendlier to the United States' own agenda. In 1973, a majority of the documents relating to brainwashing experiments and Project MKUltra were destroyed, and although 20,000 documents happened to survive, countless more were lost, and even today not much is known about what exactly the CIA learned about brainwashing and how they used that knowledge in the field. However, enough information has survived to make a useful case study out of, and while we will never know how much the CIA accomplished in their experiments, the information that is available should help you further your understanding of manipulation techniques in general.

One of the more interesting pieces of information about the CIA brainwashing experiments is that there was a wide variety of people who were experimented on. Certain people were more likely to be experimented on than others, and prostitutes, the homeless, current and former drug addicts, and incarcerated criminals were all chosen to be in the experiments. In addition, a number of CIA agents were experimented on by their own employer, and the experiments were not limited to only those of American nationality: Canadians were also targeted. In a majority of cases, the people who acted as test subjects in the experiments were unwilling participants and were never compensated for their part. Due to the extreme nature of the experiments, it made sense that the CIA would tend to choose people in society who would generally not be missed by the general public, or in the case of their own agents, people who the public was not even aware existed. More surprising, of course, is the fact that the Canadian government allowed for the CIA to experiment on their citizens, especially when most of them did not give their consent to participate.

Even more interesting than the CIA's wide selection of targets is the variety of experiments that they performed. CIA documents recovered in 1977 state that "chemical, biological, and radiological" procedures were carried out as part of MKUltra specifically, and an even greater variety of methods were used in other experiments, including electroshock procedures, various hypnosis techniques, psychological abuse, and severe isolation, sleep deprivation, and sensory deprivation processes. Most of these procedures were carried out at hospitals, universities, and prisons, and in many cases, not even the researchers knew what the experiments were really being used for. The CIA also experimented with a shockingly wide variety of drugs, including LSD, psilocybin, MDMA (more commonly known as ecstasy), salvia, a mixture of barbiturates and amphetamines, morphine, heroin, marijuana, alcohol, and other hallucinogens. The CIA had 17 goals that it wanted to achieve through the use of drugs, including attempting to speed up or slow down the aging process, causing nonreversible brain damage in targets, and even causing a target to lose control of all bodily functions and become completely paralyzed. Most of the drugs were administered to unwilling participants, many of whom were unaware that they had been put under the influence of any kind of substance.

CIA agents would even go so far as to spike their coworkers' food and drinks with LSD to see what would happen, which resulted in the death of at least one agent. Even though the results of these experiments remain largely unknown to the public, the range of the types of experiments shows the CIA's determination to see progress made.

Unlike the previous two case studies, the lessons that can be learned from the CIA brainwashing experiments might be a little bit harder for you to determine. One of the more obvious lessons to be learned from this case study is the importance of target selection. When target selection has been discussed previously within this book, the purpose has mainly been to describe which types of people are more susceptible to methods of manipulation than others. However, the CIA brainwashing experiments present another important component of target selection: the fewer connections a potential target has already, the easier they will be to manipulate. Many of the targets chosen by the CIA were people who already had a high degree of isolation from the rest of society, including prostitutes, prisoners, and drug addicts. These people certainly had fewer meaningful connections with other people than, for example, a man with a steady job or a woman with a family to take care of.

Of course, this is not saying that you should only try to manipulate prostitutes and criminals — in fact, you should try to keep your distance from those people most of the time. Instead, you should seek out people who are generally isolated from a society already, whether that is because they are unemployed or have few friends, to begin with. Another lesson to be learned from the CIA brainwashing experiments is the importance of using a number of different techniques in order to successfully manipulate your target. While the use of drugs or physical measures such as electroshocks is unacceptable techniques to use, you should never be afraid to diversify your techniques in the manipulation process. Remember that every target is slightly different and will react in different ways to different manipulation techniques, so be sure to experiment often.

Takeaways

You are ready to go out into the world and begin practicing the art of manipulation if you have not begun to do so already. Remember that these case studies are not meant as strict examples of what to do, but rather are here to help add to your preexisting knowledge of NLP, mind control, hypnosis, and brainwashing, as well as the concepts of the Dark Triad, persuasion, and deception. Keep in mind that these case studies, in particular, case studies #2 and #3, are also meant to illustrate the dangers associated with manipulation and dark psychology as a whole. Be sure to practice the techniques found in this book on a regular basis, and above all else, always be sure to act responsibly.

Conclusion

Thank you for making it through to the end of *Dark Psychology: How to Use the NLP Secret Methods of Manipulation for Social Influence, Emotional Persuasion, Deception, and Mind Control*, let's hope it was informative and able to provide you with all of the tools you need to achieve your goals whatever they may be.

The next step is to put the techniques that you have learned into practice out in the real world. Find a target that you want to manipulate and try some of your favorite techniques out, whether that means trying to control the narrative, attempting to manage your target's expectations, or making an effort to manipulate your target's beliefs. Do not expect to get everything right the first time, and do not be afraid of failure; if something goes wrong, simply learn what you can from the experience and move on to the next target. Learning a new skill is always a process, and that includes learning how to manipulate people in the world around you. If you feel that you have to, take a break from manipulation and come back to it at a later time. Frustration is never good for the learning process, and will only serve to make you want to give up altogether. As long as you keep trying, you will get there eventually. I know that I have repeated myself over and over, but remember that practice makes perfect. Once you practice long enough, you will find that you have mastered the techniques of manipulation and influence, and you will have very little difficulty in making targets bend to your will.

You should also take the time to come back to this book every so often and review the topics covered within, from the most basic concepts to the more advanced material. Even if you are practicing what you have learned on a regular basis, it is always a good idea to review in order to make sure that you are using the techniques correctly. The practice is a great thing, but only when you are not enforcing bad habits instead of developing good ones. The best way to tell good from bad is to go back and read about whatever concept you might be struggling with, instead of letting bad habits take hold for the foreseeable future. If you have any further questions about dark psychology, the art of manipulation, or any of the concepts or techniques discussed in this book, do not be afraid to research topics yourself. You might find new information that can help you to become an even better manipulator, or you might find old information presented in such a way that you understand it better. Do not assume that this book holds all of the answers, and feel free to look up any topics that you still have an interest in or concerns about.

Keep in mind that if you have made it all the way through this book to this point, then you already have far more knowledge about dark psychology and manipulation than most of the world's population is even aware exists. By getting to this point, you are already far ahead of the vast majority of people who you might try to manipulate. Feel free to try to discover the exact method of manipulation that you prefer, and do not be afraid to combine different techniques and concepts to create incredibly effective combinations. If you find the techniques that work best for you, then you will be more comfortable with manipulation as a whole, and you can work your way up to taking bigger risks and facing greater challenges. As long as you take the time to develop your newfound abilities and use them as responsibly as you can, then you will be guaranteed at least some level of success in your life. You are already a powerful and skilled manipulator, and frequent practice and occasional review sessions will help you develop into a master of dark psychology, manipulation, and influence.

www.ingramcontent.com/pod-product-compliance
Lightning Source LLC
Chambersburg PA
CBHW071630080526
44588CB00010B/1351